PICTURE BOOK
THE PRIMARY CLASSROOM

13.99

D0648243

Stuart Marriott taught in primary schools in London before taking up his present position as senior lecturer in primary education at the University of Ulster. He has written several articles about aspects of primary education, including children's fiction, and is also the author of *Primary Education and Society* (Falmer Press).

PICTURE BOOKS
IN THE
PRIMARY CLASSROOM

STUART MARRIOTT

Paul Chapman
Publishing Ltd

Paul Chapman Publishing Ltd
144 Liverpool Road
London
N1 1LA

British Library Cataloguing in Publication Data

Marriott, Stuart
  Picture books in the primary classroom.
  1. Books for primary school students. Selection & use
  I. Title
  372.132

ISBN 1−85396−144−2

Typeset by Setrite, Hong Kong
Printed by St Edmundsbury Press, Bury St Edmunds
Bound by W. H. Ware, Avon

A B C D E F 6 5 4 3 2 1

CONTENTS

Contents

INTRODUCTION

The monster ate Bernard up, every bit.
Then the monster went indoors.
'ROAR,' went the monster behind Bernard's mother.
'Not now, Bernard,' said Bernard's mother.
The monster bit Bernard's father.
'Not now, Bernard,' said Bernard's father.

Some years ago my son, then aged three, brought home a book from his nursery school. It was David McKee's *Not Now, Bernard*, and as I read it with him it made both of us laugh out loud. This was a new experience for me: the language curriculum of the primary schools in which I had taught some years earlier was almost totally dominated by rather old-fashioned reading schemes, and one thing was for sure, none of them ever made me or the children laugh!

Shortly after reading *Not Now, Bernard* I visited the local children's library, and found that this was only one of a vast number of wonderful picture books for children. In fact, as I soon discovered, in the last twenty years or so a huge range and variety of material has become easily and relatively cheaply available. From the simplest board books for pre-school children, through the thousands of books for beginning and developing readers, all the way to picture books for older children (and indeed adults, like Raymond Briggs' chilling *When the Wind Blows*), there are picture books for every reader! And not only is there quantity: much of what has been published is of the very highest quality. John Rowe Townsend, a respected authority on children's fiction, has recently described the present as a time of 'picture books in bloom'.[1]

In the course of my work I visit a lot of primary schools, and I began to look out particularly for picture books in classrooms, and to notice whether and how

'Not now, Bernard,' said Bernard's father.

Reprinted by permission of Andersen Press Limited., from *Not Now Bernard*, by David McKee.

they were being used. I found that many teachers, particularly those working with very young children, were using picture books, and with great success too. But I also found that there are some teachers who have not yet come to appreciate the value of picture books in the classroom. And so I decided that a book like this might be useful in order to encourage primary school teachers to make more use of picture books with their children. In addition, as I suggest in Chapter 4, parents have a fundamental role to play in education before and throughout the primary school years, especially in the area of literacy. I therefore hope that parents of young children will also find this kind of introduction to picture books valuable.

Generally I shall try to suggest some of the positive benefits of using books: essentially that they can make a significant contribution to children's intellectual and emotional development. Although I think picture books can be useful in a variety of classroom contexts, I shall argue that picture books are of particular value in enabling children to see reading as an inherently meaningful and enjoyable activity. I am sure that, by providing both pleasure and purpose in reading, picture books can make a substantial contribution to a more purposeful experience of the printed word for all of our children.

A central theme of this book is that teachers who wish to make the encouragement of enjoyable and meaningful reading more central to their classroom practice would find that picture books are inherently suited to such a purpose, both because of their intrinsic qualities and because most children find good picture books irresistibly attractive. Thus, although I shall suggest that picture books have relevance across the whole of the primary school curriculum and beyond, much of the discussion will concern children's language development, and especially the teaching and learning of literacy. I shall not say much about theories of how children learn to read, specific techniques of teaching reading, or the problems and difficulties of either, because there are plenty of good books devoted to such issues. Rather, I shall argue that picture books can be of great value to teachers engaged in the extremely complex task of developing children's language competence by making the activities involved both purposeful and pleasurable, which in turn may enable children to learn more quickly, and more effectively.

Much of the book (Part I, Chapters 1−6) consists of detailed discussion of the place of picture books in the primary classroom, and ways that they can be used in practice across the curriculum. In Part II (Chapters 7−11) reviews of a wide range of picture books are provided, in the hope that teachers may find material that is both attractive and also appropriate for children of different ages, attainments and interests. Appendices, indexes and a bibliography can be found at the end of the book.

I would like to thank a number of people for their help while I was writing this book. Firstly, my thanks to Chris McIvor and her colleagues at the Coleraine Public Library for their interest in the whole project and for their time and effort in providing copies of picture books for me. I am also grateful to the staff and children of Mill Strand Integrated Primary School, Portrush (especially Carolyn Moore), and Windmill Integrated Primary School, Dungannon, for all their help. Kay Ballantine, Bill Hart, Dolores O'Kane and Bill O'Neill were also very helpful and made useful comments on parts of the text. And finally, my thanks to Nicholas and Aidan Marriott, two omnivorous readers and opinionated critics of picture books, and to their mother who has tried to put it all into practice.

Notes and References

1. Townsend, J. R. *Written for Children* (3rd edn), Harmondsworth, Penguin, 1987.

Picture Books Mentioned in the Text

Briggs, R. *When the Wind Blows*, Penguin.
McKee, D. *Not Now, Bernard*, Andersen/Sparrow.

PART I
PICTURE BOOKS IN THE PRIMARY CLASSROOM

1
WHY USE PICTURE BOOKS?

Purposes for Reading

It is hard to imagine what it is like to be an adult in the modern world who is totally unable to read or write. Quite apart from the obvious difficulties of managing everyday life, how would it feel? How could one cope with an inability to achieve what everyone else appears to be able to do so effortlessly? For almost everyone in our society, the ability to read and write at least at a basic level is completely taken for granted, and the illiterate is at best pitied and at worst despised. So fundamental is literacy, indeed, that whatever else schools and teachers do, public expectations that the process of education involves the teaching and learning of reading and writing are also completely taken for granted. Such expectations are of course shared by teachers, and there is unsurprising evidence[1] that reading is regarded by primary teachers as being the most important of all the curriculum areas.

Because of such assumptions it is very rare that any challenge is made to the view that the teaching of literacy is one of the central concerns of schools in general, and primary schools in particular; nor does anyone ever disagree with the assertion that one of the main reasons that children attend primary schools at all is to learn to read and write. And so we do not often need to consider explicitly the purposes for which we teach literacy, or the reasons why it is so vital that children should learn to read skilfully and fluently: the reasons and purposes seem obvious to us as teachers, and equally obvious to everybody else. Nevertheless it may be worth spelling them out very briefly since they provide a context for later discussion of the role and value of picture books in the classroom.

A number of slightly different classifications of reasons for reading have been devised by researchers and scholars, but we do not at present need to go into much detail. For our purposes a brief outline of just five broad categories can be considered.

Utilitarian Purposes

Firstly there are what one might call the utilitarian or functional purposes of reading. In order to cope without major disruption to one's everyday life, one has to be able to read car number plates, road signs, cookery recipes, bus timetables, safety notices, medical cards, tax and insurance forms, advertising material, labels on tins and bottles, and so on. In an almost literal sense, reading at this level is necessary to be able to survive and function at all in an advanced industrial society.

Vocational Purposes

A more or less sophisticated level of reading ability is required for almost all occupations, and thus one might delineate a set of vocational reasons for learning to read: in order to be an effective shop assistant, typist, engineer or whatever, being able to read is crucial to the job. Rare individuals prosper occupationally in spite of severe disabilities in literacy, but such cases are very unusual (so much so as to be newsworthy). Much more commonly the illiterate or semi-literate is more or less unemployable.

Educational Purposes

For teachers probably the most obvious purpose of reading is that it is almost always necessary for education, for learning anything else: all subjects depend on language and thus in part on reading. Despite advances in audio-visual and technological communication, such as the increasing availability of electronic sources of information like Oracle and Prestel, for the present (and the foreseeable future) 'the culture of the school is largely the culture of the book'.[2] Not only is this the case, of course, for the kinds of formal education which occur in school classrooms, but it is also true of the informal learning which children and adults engage in through reading newspapers or magazines or personal letters, and the recreational reading of information material in order to find out about gardening or car maintenance or any other interest. In all such ways, some relatively trivial but some fundamental, individuals can engage with the arguments, ideas, theories and knowledge current in the society of which they are members.

Personal and Social Purposes

Fourthly, there are what might be called personal and social reasons for reading. Robert Protherough, for example, argues that books, especially fiction, can:

- Aid personal development and self-understanding by presenting situations and characters with which our own can be compared, and by giving the chance to test out motives and decisions.
- Extend experience and knowledge of life ('broaden the mind' and 'widen the horizons') by introducing us to other kinds of people, places, periods and situations.[3]

This purpose for reading is less easy to define precisely than some of the others. However, it may be plausibly argued that reading can stimulate the imagination, the intellect and the emotions; it can help us to speculate and hypothesize about what is possible, and enable us to shape present experience and organize events in the past. A good reason for reading is thus to enable us or assist us to come to terms with our own lives, to make some sense of our everyday social world, by implicitly comparing it with realities (whether fictional or non-fictional) constructed by authors.

Such reading can also enable us to become members of a literary community, engaging in forms of literary dialogue and thus experiencing the world from new vantage points. As Barbara Hardy has suggested, narrative can be seen as a 'primary act of mind', not an immature state out of which we grow into understanding life as it really is: 'We do not grow out of telling stories.'[4]

Reading for Pleasure

Finally, reading can be enjoyable: it can be fun. Not only may reading enable us to operate effectively within our society in a variety of ways, not only may it help us to come to terms with ourselves and our personal and social relationships, but it can also provide a source of endless pleasure and relaxation. Reading can make us laugh and it can make us cry; it can take us away from our everyday chores and dreary routines to adventure and excitement; it can enable us to be rich or powerful or famous or beautiful (or even all four!); and it can allow us to escape to a more colourful, more dramatic or more congenial world. For some readers this is the most important reason of all for reading, and perhaps for many it is the one which leads them to reach for a book with eagerness and anticipation.

Children and Reading

As I suggested earlier, the details of such a classification are not vital at present; the point is that we all have, consciously or subconsciously, a variety of powerful and entirely valid reasons and purposes which lie behind our assumptions that children must learn to read. But while they are all significant to some degree to us as adults and teachers, perhaps some of them make little real sense to children, especially those just starting school. In fact, as Reid showed some years ago on the basis of interviews with five year olds, reading may well be for them 'a mysterious experience, to which they come with only the vaguest of expectancies'.[5] The children Reid talked to had little idea of what reading was going to be like, or of what the activity consisted, or of the purpose of it. By the age of seven to nine, the fifty children interviewed by Southgate *et al.* in their fascinating research study[6] were beginning to develop theories of the purposes of reading, but still rather tentatively. In general, the children understood being a good reader as the mastery of word recognition skills and the ability to proceed quickly through a graded reading scheme, but many seemed ignorant of or resistant to any wider purposes. Not all the children interviewed could provide any reasons at all for reading, and several more could say nothing specific (or in a few cases denied that reading was of any use!). Thirty-four specific reasons were suggested: eleven children saw reading as useful mainly to help with spelling or writing activities, which as Southgate notes is a kind of circular justification; twelve children said that reading was important for further study or learning, and eight that it was useful for acquiring information; only three children suggested that reading could be seen as being for pleasure.

If these are typical cases, then, whatever else children learn about reading they do not seem to be convinced of the fifth reason for reading outlined above: it does not seem to them a particularly enjoyable activity. Why not? Why is it that an activity which can give such pleasure is apparently rarely seen by young children as of intrinsic value? Inevitably this leads us into at least a brief consideration of aspects of the initial teaching of reading, since it is at this stage that basic attitudes towards reading, as well as the various skills and competencies, begin to be developed.

There is no shortage of ideas, prescriptions and theories about the teaching of reading; indeed, they are overwhelming in their scope and complexity.[7] Fortunately, perhaps, we do not need to discuss them in great detail here. However, over the last few years a rather new debate has arisen which is closely connected to the reasons and purposes outlined earlier; or at least to the question of their relative priority in the context of young children's learning, given that they are all important to some degree. Few would disagree with the view that we hope that children will become eager, skilful and voracious readers, but how is this to be achieved?

Learning Reading: the 'Real Books' Debate

Some practising teachers of young children, notably Liz Waterland and Jill Bennett,[8] have recently argued that many children never become real readers in any meaningful sense. They suggest that such children can cope with functional reading, but do not turn easily and naturally to books. In particular, they do not view books as a source of intrinsic pleasure and enjoyment. These children would not, if they were asked, agree with Waterland's comment that 'Books are an end in themselves: they are the reason for reading, not merely the objects by which people are enabled to learn to read',[9] since their experience is to the contrary. Such children, they argue, can be found in primary schools and in great numbers in secondary schools; and indeed, according to some evidence,[10] by the age of 14+ regular voluntary book reading (that is, apart from what is required for school purposes) is rather a minority interest.

Waterland argues that such relative lack of commitment to reading is at least partly due to the long-term effects of methods and materials employed in infant classrooms which treat reading as a series of somewhat isolated skills and sub-skills, to be tackled both sequentially and hierarchically. Thus, for example, as has often been pointed out in relation to the early stages of traditional reading schemes, the emphasis on structure, on repetition and on controlled vocabulary is so strong that meaning, let alone a real sense of story, can sometimes be almost completely lost. Here is the text on six consecutive pages from the first book in one well-known reading scheme, not untypical of its type:

> Here is Peter and here is Jane.
> Peter is here and Jane is here.
> Here is the dog.
> Here is Jane and here is the dog.
> Jane likes the dog and Peter likes the dog.
> The dog likes Jane and the dog likes Peter.[11]

And so on, almost indefinitely. As Wade has argued, such texts bear 'little relationship to the language as the child has learned to use it. Additionally, they make of narrative something apart from life as it is lived.'[12]

The result of the concentrated use of these kinds of rather sterile early reading books and the failure to enable children to encounter other forms of literary material can be that, while children more or less successfully decode the written word, they do not develop into eager and enthusiastic readers. As Clarke has suggested on the basis of her research into the characteristics and experiences of a group of fluent young readers:

> The teacher concerned with the young child and the beginning reader . . . has tended to have too little appreciation of the effects that her initial approach to the reading situation may have on the children's later progress, on their motivation and appreciation of reading as a language based activity. She has also been too little aware of the complexity and range of skills that even the beginning reader brings to the reading situation.[13]

Or as Trelease puts it, rather more pithily, if also somewhat simplistically: 'The problem is that we have concentrated exclusively on teaching the child how to ᵣᵉad, and we have forgotten to teach him to want to read.'[14]

Waterland goes on to argue that becoming a reader is a process of learning to construct meaning through interaction with a text. This interaction is two-way: the reader brings to the text as much as he or she takes from it. Such meaning making is fundamental to the process of learning to read, and not an end-state to be achieved after all the skills have been mastered.

An analogy may help to make the point. Consider one possible approach to teaching children to play football. We could say to children, in effect, 'Sit down in a classroom and learn the laws of the game. We'll test you to make sure you really understand the rules, and when you've convinced us then, and only then, you can go out and kick a ball.' Intuitively, this seems a fairly daft way of proceeding. We would probably think that children learn to play football more effectively by taking a ball out and kicking it around from the start, and thus immediately approximating the behaviour of real footballers. And of course, at the same time, with the help of teachers or others who are knowledgeable, children can learn about the skills and tactics (and rules) of the game as they go along. Such an approach, viewing the learner as an apprentice, an unskilled practitioner, from the beginning, is the way much learning occurs both for children and for adults (as anyone who has ever learnt to drive a car will testify!).[15] This is not, of course, to deny that the football (or driving) teacher has a central role; rather, his or her task becomes that of developing and refining skills, and enabling the learner to understand more of the principles of the activity, all in the context of the practical experience of the learner.

Consideration of the way in which children learn to talk in the first two or three years of life is also instructive, even though the parallels with reading are not in my view as close as is sometimes asserted. Children learn to speak fluently and intelligibly without any formal instruction in the rules of grammar or syntax; rather, the teaching and learning implicit in their everyday social life enables them to make sense for themselves of the rules by which language operates. When my very young son was being put to bed one night he said, 'Daddy put the dark on.' He had presumably heard adults talking about putting the light on and was generalizing and extending from this experience. As it happened he got it wrong because we usually say 'put the light off' rather than 'put the dark on'. However, the incident illustrates the way in which the conventions of language that we use are actively processed by the child, not in isolation but through the process of interaction with other people. My son's confusion arose because he had learnt a rule of the English language through dialogue with adults and peers, but was applying it inappropriately. He was not mistaken because his parents had failed to teach him grammar!

Thus the learner can behave in ways which approximate to the behaviour of a skilled adult speaker, footballer, car driver, or whatever, from the start. He or she can then gradually refine skills and techniques through prolonged practice and experience (and reflection on that experience) often with the help of a teacher; this may of course include the formal learning of the rules of the Highway Code or the laws of Association Football, or whatever. In such ways the learner can increasingly achieve the level of attainment of the fully competent.

The same, it can be argued, is true in the case of learning to read. The child can be viewed as an apprentice reader from the beginning because he or she can, admittedly unskilfully and imperfectly, approach reading in the same kind of way as an adult reader. So, rather than viewing the child as a sort of literary and linguistic vacuum which has to be filled up by the teacher with knowledge about the reading process and skills and strategies to use before letting him or her loose on books, the apprenticeship model demands that the learner is encouraged to to read worthwhile books and stories from day one. In addition, of course, skilful and sensitive teaching is needed: as Waterland makes clear, the approach requires even greater professional expertise from the teacher than traditional practices and techniques.

Teaching Reading: Implications for Classroom Practice

While the work of Waterland and others, and the theoretical framework which lies behind it, is much more complex and carefully worked out than this rather sketchy summary suggests, it will suffice for present purposes. Such ideas and the consequent implications for classroom practice have generated fierce controversy recently, including some enthusiastic espousal and some vehement denial: 'Modern theorists are talking rubbish — reading schemes are necessary' is a fairly typical recent example.[16]

Such a cycle of affirmation and contradiction, based largely on feeling and intuition rather than research evidence, is obviously unsatisfactory. However, as far as I know, no adequate comparative research work yet exists. Clearly, providing evidence demonstrating the relative success or failure of early reading teaching by traditional means and by the methods and techniques advocated by Waterland and others is a task of huge complexity and difficulty; indeed, whether the argument is provable one way or the other must be doubtful. In the meantime it may be that until hard evidence exists (if it ever does) teachers will wish to stick with methods and strategies, albeit modified somewhat, that are familiar and reliable; after all, the vast majority of children at present do learn to read successfully.

Fortunately, however, a final conclusion can be deferred because, whether the theoretical analysis and practical implications of Waterland's ideas are accepted in their entirety, or in part, or hardly at all, what is important for our present discussion is the stress on reading as an activity which is centred on the construction of meaning. In Gordon Wells' phrase, children are 'meaning makers'[17] every time they open a book, and thus learning to read can be seen, at least in part, as a matter of developing children's meaning-making capabilities. The process of learning to read undoubtedly contributes to children's ability to make sense of the social world they inhabit, and thus to the development of their intellectual capacities in general. Similarly, we learn to read and to read better by using our experience to construct meaning in the texts that we look at. As has recently been noted in official guidance relating to the National Curriculum, 'When we read something we make sense of it for ourselves, not just by "decoding" but by bringing our own experience and understanding to it.'[18] Thus the process of reading is cyclical: experience enables us to make sense of our reading; reading enables us to make sense of our experience.

For these reasons teachers may regard it as important that children should be enabled to find meaning and purpose in the activities that they undertake. In other words, one of the fundamental tasks of the teacher is to help children to understand even in the earliest days not only what they should do but why they should do it, in order that they may make sense for themselves of the activities they engage in. For the teacher to provide children with reasons and purposes for reading, and to encourage them to view learning to read as a meaningful activity, is thus not an optional extra but likely to be highly significant to their progress. And so one does not have to agree with all the arguments of the proponents of 'real books' to accept, as McKenzie has argued,[19] that growth in the ability to read is more likely to flourish in a supportive, literate environment in which the motivation to read is purposeful, active and meaningful.

If all this makes sense, it is of course possible and quite legitimate to provide opportunities and contexts for children to learn a little about utilitarian, vocational or other reasons for reading. Whether young children can have any real comprehension of such purposes seems more doubtful: children's experience is so limited that this may prove difficult. As Meek says:

> We know why reading and writing are important, but our reasoning about good jobs, for instance, cannot impress a beginner. You can't tell a five year old about the importance of literacy; you can only help him to discover the fun of it.[20]

Perhaps, then, the fifth reason for reading outlined above is one which is particularly useful and important for the teacher, since it is not at all difficult for children to comprehend. Clearly even the youngest and most immature reader can make sense of the activity in terms of whether or not it is exciting and enjoyable at his or her individual intellectual and emotional level. Enjoyment is thus one obvious rationale, a reason that can realistically be shared by both beginners and mature adult readers. It may therefore be that teachers could usefully lay greater stress on reading for pleasure to provide for children a powerful purpose for the literary activities they engage in. And, of course, reading for enjoyment is also of great importance because activities which children find pleasurable and meaningful are much more likely to develop positive attitudes towards the reading process itself. Although there are no certainties in this area, it seems likely that children with such positive attitudes will in fact read more and more widely, and that therefore all the other purposes of reading will also be achieved more readily.

In such ways the ideas of Waterland and Bennett and of the theorists whose work supports them have provided the impetus for a generally increased prominence and priority being given to the fifth purpose of reading outlined earlier, as a stimulating and enjoyable activity for its own sake. And thus even a writer like Betty Root, in a paper highly critical of the 'real books' movement, nevertheless concludes that the 'emphasis has to be on the children's ability and desire to read with pleasure'.[21]

The views of Waterland, Bennett and others collectively form just one set of ideas about the initial teaching of reading, and there are a multiplicity of other approaches, methods and theories. Opinions may and do legitimately differ as to whether teaching reading using only 'real books', or for that matter any other single approach, can sensibly be regarded as the one true faith. In particular, teachers may disagree as to whether in classroom situations one or more reading schemes and the ideas and practices traditionally associated with them are essential and central to the teaching of reading; or whether they should be used as a core around which other materials can be used; or whether they are anathema, to be banished from every display case and stock cupboard. Teachers individually and collectively will justifiably make such judgements on the basis of their professional knowledge, expertise and understanding, and it is no part of my purpose in this book to deny the validity of such a decision-making process. But whatever the decision may be, however it is arrived at, and for whatever reasons, my claim is that it can still be powerfully argued that children's fiction in all its range and variety is central to teaching and learning reading in the primary classroom. As I have suggested, this is essentially because the powerful narratives of the best children's literature have two functions which are vital for fluent and effective reading: they make it possible for the child to work at the construction of meaning (which is fundamental to all learning); and they provide the motivation which is crucial to the development of attitudes that foster life-long reading.

Conclusion: The Value of Picture Books

It may be that Beard's summary of this series of related issues is a sensible view of this area of reading at the present time. He argues that for a variety of reasons asibility of a full-scale 'real books' approach to the teaching of reading in primary schools is as yet unproven. But he goes on to say:

> However, there are many arguments for saying that today's picture books are so rich and varied that they deserve to play as big a part as possible in children's language and literacy development, in the pre-school as well as the school years.[22]

In other words, one does not have to be a committed supporter of the real books approach to accept that the use of children's literature in general and picture books in particular is not a mere frill to be banished to the edges of classroom work, but is of importance in the actual process of learning to read, and therefore deserves to be taken very seriously.

Picture books are relevant to this discussion, then, for three main reasons:

- They can contribute to the development of children's intellectual abilities: picture books can provide the raw material for children's meaning making.
- They can provide powerful motivation for children to learn to read, and to become mature and fluent readers.
- They can enable children to develop their competencies in language: children can acquire skills of reading, of talking and of listening through the use of picture books.

While these are perhaps the main attractions of picture books for the primary school teacher, there are at least two more reasons for their use which are also worth bearing in mind, and which will be considered in more detail later:

- They can contribute to children's social experience: picture books are inherently sociable and provide opportunities for co-operative activities.
- They can help to develop children's aesthetic sense: picture books can be seen as an art form straddling the worlds of literature and visual arts, and thus as being of intrinsic and unique interest.

In Chapter 2 these reasons for valuing picture books in the primary classroom are discussed further in the context of some notable examples.

Notes and References

1. Ashton, P., 'Primary teachers' aims 1969–77', in Simon, B. and Willcocks, J. (eds.), *Research and Practice in the Primary Classroom*, London, Routledge & Kegan Paul, 1981.

2. Heeks, P., *Choosing and Using Books in the First School*, London, Macmillan, 1981, p. 109.

3. Protherough, R., *Developing Response to Fiction*. Milton Keynes, Open University Press, 1983, p. 7.

4. Hardy, B., 'Narrative as a primary act of mind', in Meek, M. *et al.* (eds.), *The Cool Web: The Pattern of Children's Reading*, London, Bodley Head, 1977, p. 14.

5. Reid, J. F., 'Learning to think about reading', reprinted in Melnik, A. and Merritt, J. (eds.), *Reading Today and Tomorrow*, University of London Press, 1972, p. 211.

6. Southgate, V. *et al.*, *Extending Beginning Reading*, London, Heinemann, 1981.

7. For a comprehensive review, see Beard, R., *Developing Reading 3–13*, London, Hodder & Stoughton, 1987.

8. Waterland, L., *Read With Me* (2nd edn), Stroud, Thimble Press, 1988; J. Bennett, *Learning to Read with Picture Books* (3rd edn), Stroud, Thimble Press, 1985.

9. Waterland, *op. cit.*, p. 41.

10. See, for example, Whitehead, F. *et al.*, *Children and their Books*, London, Macmillan, 1975. The more recent APU survey, *Attitudes to Reading at Age 15* (DES, 1987), states that 'for about a quarter of the pupils in their last year at school, reading is decidedly not a regular source of pleasure'.

11. Murray, W., *Play With Us* (Key Words Reading Scheme), Loughborough, Ladybird, 1964.

12. Wade, B., 'Reading rickets and the uses of story', *English in Education*, Vol. 16, no. 3, 1982, p. 36.

13. Clark, M., *Young Fluent Readers,* London, Heinemann, 1976, p. 98.

14. Trelease, J., *The Read-Aloud Handbook*, Harmondsworth, Penguin, 1984, p. 30.

15. A sophisticated yet attractively easy-to-read book about how children learn is Donaldson, M., *Children's Minds*, Fontana, 1978. The implications of Donaldson's and others' work for literacy teaching have been discussed by many writers: see, for example, Spink, J., *Children as Readers*, London, Clive Bingley, 1989.

16. Nichols, J., 'In my view', *Child Education*, September 1988; cf. Hynds, J., 'In pursuit of a little understanding', *Books for Keeps*, no. 52, September 1988.

17. Wells, G., *The Meaning Makers: Children Learning Language and Using Language to Learn*. London, Hodder & Stoughton, 1987.

18. National Curriculum Council, *English Key Stage 1: Non-Statutory Guidance*, York, National Curriculum Council, 1989, p. C8, section 6.1.

19. McKenzie, M., *Journeys into Literacy,* Huddersfield, Schofield & Sims, 1986.

20. Meek, M., *Learning to Read*, London, Bodley Head, 1982, p. 18.

21. Root, B., *In Defence of Reading Schemes*, University of Reading School of Education Reading and Language Information Centre, 1986, p. 3.

22. Beard, *op. cit.*, p. 180.

2
PICTURE BOOKS AND BECOMING
A READER

Picture books form only a small proportion of the literature available for children, and there are obviously many other types and styles of material which can play a significant part in children's intellectual development in general and reading development in particular. For example, as well as the whole of children's literature, in itself a vast range of material, there are also huge resources of oral culture: nursery rhymes, songs and poems, jingles, jokes, riddles and so on, which are of great value (see the remarkable and fascinating work of Iona and Peter Opie who devoted many years to collecting and publishing such material).[1] For children beyond the initial stages of reading, not only story books of all kinds but many of the readable and fascinating information books now available can and should play increasingly important roles. Picture books, then, form only one resource among many, but a particularly accessible and attractive one.

There is a wealth of wonderful picture books in print which are especially suited to the needs of the youngest and least confident readers, although, as I shall argue a little later, picture books also have a place in the language curriculum of older and/or more skilful readers. But what is unique about picture books? How do they work? What can children do with them? What specifically can picture books contribute to children's cognitive development, and in particular what part do they play in the language curriculum of the primary classroom? Perhaps the easiest way of beginning to answer such questions is to look at a few examples of picture books of different types and styles.

Sunshine

Sunshine by Jan Ormerod was first published in a hardback version by Viking Kestrel in 1981, and is now available in Picture Puffin paperback. It is a story of a small girl who gets up very early, and wakes her parents. Dad makes breakfast for the little girl, after initially burning the toast, and takes tea up to Mum. Dad is soon immersed in the newspaper, while Mum goes back to sleep. Meanwhile the little girl gets washed and dressed, and only then looks at the clock. When she shows it to Mum and Dad panic ensues as they rush about getting ready to go out, while the little girl stands rather smugly waiting for them. Eventually everyone is ready, and Mum and the little girl leave the house together.

Sunshine is a book without words. Somehow to say this implies a deficiency, something lacking, but in this case it is certainly not so. There is simply no need for text because the story stands on its own. And it is a story that is told very skilfully. There is a leisurely build-up: breakfast in bed followed by two double-page spreads in which the little girl is getting dressed. The slow pace builds up a kind of tension and heightens the sense of panic as the adults rush about, which is followed in turn by a much more relaxed and gentle winding down as Dad kisses the little girl goodbye and Mum brushes her hair before taking her off to school.

The humour of the story is much appreciated by children (and adults). Perhaps it is the idea that the little girl has put one over on Mum and Dad, as it were, that is irresistibly attractive to children! Or perhaps it is because the events of the story are such a common experience for all of us, even in the best regulated households! In any event, the book is both attractive to and enjoyed by young children. And so, like all the best picture books, reading *Sunshine* is such fun that many children would be motivated to look for more books which provide the same pleasure (such as the sequel, *Moonlight*).

This is all very well, but leaving aside the intrinsic pleasures of a book like *Sunshine*, what do young children actually learn from the book? Firstly, it is important to point out how the book provides experience in reading pictures. All illustrations in picture books, and indeed all works of visual art, incorporate conventions which have to be learnt (in the same way as the reader has to learn the conventions of English spelling). For example, on the pages where there are no less than eighteen pictures of the little girl taking off her night clothes and getting dressed, the reader has to understand that these are not pictures of different children, but are all pictures of the same little girl, linked together in a sequence from left to right through time. Similarly, there are conventions about scale (objects are drawn smaller than in reality, and may vary in size depending on the size of the picture frame) and perspective (large objects may be depicted as small to indicate distance) and so on. Even the techniques used by illustrators to indicate movement (such as the posture of the body and the position of arms and legs) and the various ways that artists provide the impression of three dimensions while using only two, have to be learnt.

All these conventions seem very obvious to adults because we learnt them a long time ago and now take them for granted. But they are not nearly so obvious

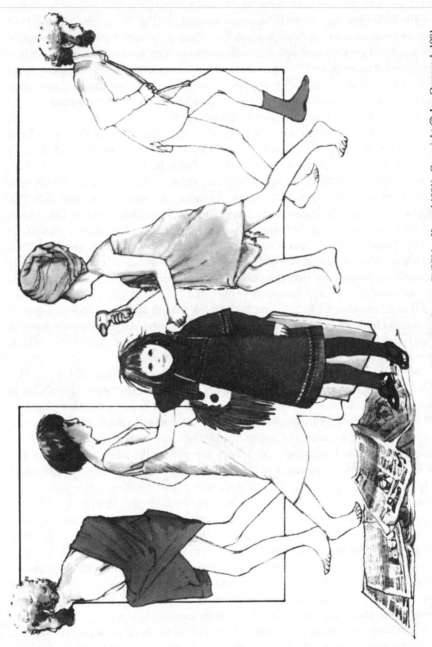

to a very young child, and it is important that children come to terms with them not only in order to enjoy a book like *Sunshine* and thus to begin to appreciate the nature and pleasures of the visual arts in general, but also because the conventions of symbolic representation are fundamental to so much learning: very similar principles are used in maps, plans, diagrams, models and so on.[2]

As well as providing experiences which are crucial to reading pictures, *Sunshine* enables the child to practise skills and techniques which are central to reading the written word. For example, the book invites the child to anticipate and predict what will happen to the characters as the book proceeds, and so to construct the story for him or herself. So children can learn something of the nature of stories from books like this. They can discover that a story has a beginning, a middle and an end, and that such parts are functionally related to create a whole. They can see too how the story builds up to a climax, and is then resolved in a satisfying way. But perhaps the most important contribution of a book like *Sunshine* to the process of learning to read is the amount of talk it generates. Whether it is two children looking at the book together, or an adult reading the story with an individual child, it demands and gets reader response – questions, comments, exclamations, comparisons, anecdotes, laughter. If, as suggested earlier, reading is essentially about making meaning, then *Sunshine* provides a framework for discussion which enables that process to occur readily, quickly and enjoyably.

Rosie's Walk

Rosie's Walk by Pat Hutchins was published in 1970 by Bodley Head, and is also available in paperback from Picture Puffin. Only thirty-two words make up the whole text: 'Rosie the hen went for a walk across the yard around the pond over the haycock past the mill through the fence under the beehives and got back in time for dinner.' The whole point of the book is that the text alone does not tell the story: just behind Rosie and following her all along her walk is a fox who is about to pounce. But somehow or other disaster strikes the fox at every crucial moment – and he ends up himself being chased away over the hill by a swarm of bees. The delight of the book for children seems to be in Rosie's apparent obliviousness to her danger: author and reader can collaborate in the joke at Rosie's expense (and the fox's, of course!).

The pictures are big and bold and somewhat stylized in red, yellow, brown and green, but fit the sense of fun in the book perfectly; the words too are large and clear, and of course very simple. Even more importantly, text and illustrations are interdependent: they work together to create a reading experience which is more powerful than either could achieve in isolation. All the very best picture books provide this sense that both words and pictures are essential, neither

Reprinted with permission from *Rosie's Walk*, Pat Hutchins, 1970, The Bodley Head.

giving the impression of having been tacked on almost as an afterthought. So *Rosie's Walk* triumphantly succeeds in achieving some of the most important criteria for any work of fiction in any genre: it is enjoyable certainly, but also complete and coherent, forming a satisfying whole.

As well as the conventions about pictures mentioned earlier, as adults we also take for granted many rules about how written text should be read: for example, that we have to read from the front of the book to the back and not vice versa, and that pages should be read from top to bottom and from left to right. We have learned that the same words sometimes appear in different typefaces, and even that some books have dedications (as here: 'For Wendy and Stephen'). *Rosie's Walk*, like other picture books, teaches these crucial conventions, and indeed Rosie herself 'moves' from left to right, in the same direction as the print on the page. Margaret Meek explores such apparently trivial details in her recent and fascinating analysis of the interaction between readers and picture books, when she discusses reading *Rosie's Walk* with a child named Ben:

The print on this page is *Pat Hutchins, ROSIE'S WALK, The Bodley Head, London, Sydney, Toronto*. Most accomplished readers turn this page, taking the conventions of

Rosie the hen went for a walk

publishing for granted . . . When did you learn that you don't read these words as part of the story?[3]

Equally importantly, in *Rosie's Walk* what is not said is at least as important as what is: children can thus learn to attend to what the author is not saying but implying. To be able to do so is a crucial ability of the skilled reader. Further, children can begin to learn that the context of the words can contribute to a reading experience, and can be used to help to predict and to understand the story. In this case the context is provided by the pictures, obviously, but even the youngest reader can bring expectations (such as about the behaviour of hens and foxes) to the text which may be confirmed or denied, but in any event help to make sense of the story. Note too the incidental information: children can learn a little more about the characteristics of hens, foxes, ponds, rakes, bees, flour mills, etc. quite easily and naturally.

More generally, books like *Rosie's Walk* can help to develop children's capacity to wonder and to enquire and to try to make sense of their world; they encourage children to speculate and hypothesize, to think through questions like 'What would happen if . . .?' and 'How can you be sure that . . .?' and 'Why

That's the third and last time I'm asking you whether you want a drink, Shirley

Reprinted with permission from *Come Away From The Water, Shirley*, John Burningham, 1977, Jonathan Cape.

is it that ...?' In all such ways, picture books can contribute to children's construction of meaning as well as their ability to decode the printed word.

Come Away from the Water, Shirley

While many, perhaps most, picture books are intended for beginning readers, there are also plenty which older primary school children can enjoy. An excellent example is John Burningham's *Come Away from the Water, Shirley*, which was originally published in 1977 by Jonathan Cape, and is also available in a Picture Lion paperback version. On the left-hand side of each of ten double-page spreads, Mum and Dad are sitting in deckchairs on the beach. They do not move much throughout the book: Mum does some knitting, and pours out a drink from a thermos; Dad reads the paper and later slumps back in a lengthy snooze. On each page too, Mum issues one of a series of instructions, requests and complaints to the daughter ('Mind you don't get any of that filthy tar on your nice new shoes'; 'Don't stroke that dog, Shirley, you don't know where he's been'; and so on). But on the right-hand side of the pages, Shirley is depicted rowing off to a pirate ship, walking the plank, escaping with a map showing hidden treasure, and digging up a huge box of gold and jewels. Shirley's

romantic and flamboyant adventures are appropriately pictured in glowing technicolour, while the illustrations of static Mum and Dad seem pale and almost monochrome in comparison.

While younger children certainly enjoy Shirley's adventures, the main point of the book which older readers appreciate is of course the dramatic and ironic contrast on each page between the relatively tedious and routine day at the beach and the power of Shirley's imagination to lift herself out of the humdrum and into a vivid daydream. For example, as Mum calls in exasperation (just like the reader's Mum), 'That's the third and last time I'm asking you whether you want a drink, Shirley', Shirley herself is singlehandedly laying into a motley crew of vicious pirates.

There is probably no need to labour the point that the experience of reading a book like *Come Away from the Water, Shirley* is of much educational significance. For example, quite apart from their intrinsic value in providing aesthetic and emotional experience, such books have great advantages in terms of classroom practice as they are especially suited to forms of shared reading. Groups of children of differing abilities and attainments can look at a picture book together in a way that is difficult with text alone. Members of such groups bring varied experience to the book, but all can take something valuable from it. Reading is no longer only a rather isolated and individual business, but is co-operative. And, of course, a good picture book provides endless opportunities for discussion about the story and its implications, in small groups or in the class as a whole, and at a variety of levels of sophistication, as will be considered in more detail later.

Such books also contribute to children's reading development. To quote Benton and Fox, writing specifically about *Come Away from the Water, Shirley*, each time children look at the pictures and the text they are

> simultaneously exploring the details within the still frame *per se*, and also interpreting the frame itself as a detail within the whole narrative. This experience of, at once, making local meanings and fitting them into the larger pattern of the story is the imaginative exercise performed by all readers — whether of text or picture books — and constitutes *the* essential element of reading development.[4]

The Jolly Postman

The preceding remarks apply with equal force to a fourth picture book, Janet and Allan Ahlberg's *The Jolly Postman*, which is well worth a brief discussion. It was published in 1986 by Heinemann; no paperback version is yet available. Like all of the Ahlbergs' work, *The Jolly Postman* is both of the highest literary and artistic quality, and also very popular with children. It is not easy to do justice to what is a most unusual and attractive picture book in a short summary, but essentially the book follows a postman delivering letters to various characters from nursery rhymes and fairy stories. The really innovative touch is that running alongside the story of the postman, the book contains the letters, postcards, party invitations and so on, each inside its own appropriately addressed envelope, to be taken out and looked at by the reader. There is a letter from Goldilocks to the three bears, a postcard from Jack to the beanstalk giant, a mail order advertisement for the wicked witch, a letter to the big bad wolf from solicitors representing Little Red Riding Hood and the three little pigs, and so on.

One of the most useful qualities of *The Jolly Postman* is that it can be appreciated by children of almost any age or reading competence, really from beginning reader to adult; there are so many layers to the book that it can be enjoyed at many different levels. For example, the humour is very varied: from the near slapstick of the postman avoiding drinking the cup of tea made by the witch ('it was green!') to the more subtle humour of the letter from Meeny, Miny, Mo & Co., solicitors, to the big bad wolf:

> Messrs Three Little Pigs Ltd are now firmly resolved to sue for damages. Your offer of shares in a turnip or apple-picking business is declined, and all this huffing and puffing will get you nowhere.

As with the other books, *The Jolly Postman* invites, almost demands, talk and discussion, and provides opportunities for narration and retelling. Even the very

So the Bears read the letter (except Baby Bear),
  The Postman drank his tea
And what happened next
  We'll very soon see.

Dear Mr and Mrs Bear
          and Baby Bear,
     I am very sory indeed that I
cam into your house
and ate Baby Bears
porij. Mummy says I am a bad girl.
I hardly eat any porij when she cooks
it she says. Daddy says he will
mend the littel chair.

          Love from
          Goldilocks

P.S. Baby Bear can come to my
party if he likes. Ther will be 3
kinds of jelly and a conjoora.

Reprinted with permission from
The Jolly Postman, Janet and Allan
Ahlberg, 1986, William Heinemann
Ltd.

youngest children can follow the simple and repetitive story of the postman's day with its delightfully appropriate illustrations, and can enjoy taking the letters and other material out of the envelopes to look at. Older children can also enjoy relating the contents of the letters to the stories of famous nursery characters that they know so well. And the most mature readers can appreciate the way in which so many strands of the stories of early childhood are revisited, alluded to, developed and then tied together in a coherent whole.

In the case of *The Jolly Postman* then, to use Benton and Fox's comments again, the reader has to work not only at interpreting the 'still frame' in terms of the structure of the whole picture book, but also at making sense of the book itself within a framework of even more extensive meanings – a very sophisticated skill indeed!

The Highwayman

Although some of the picture books discussed so far can be and are enjoyed by older primary school children, it may finally be of interest to look at an illustrated version of Alfred Noyes' famous poem *The Highwayman*, which seems to be intended for children of eleven or twelve and over; probably only the most mature children in primary school would fully appreciate it.

The authors of the recently published proposals for English in the National Curriculum have recently and wisely remarked that 'picture books are not just for the young'.[5] However, many older children seem to resist picture books of any kind on the grounds that they are babyish and rather beneath their dignity. It is perhaps ironic that the children who one minute are rejecting picture books are to be seen a moment later immersed in comics! (And, of course, authors such as Raymond Briggs and Hergé have adopted some of the techniques of comics for their picture books.) There are some teachers too who apparently believe that once children have 'learnt to read' there is no longer any need for pictures. Benton and Fox note rather sorrowfully that for nine to fourteen year olds

> in the earnest world of school, picture books are given scant regard, children's visual education goes underground into comics and sideways into television, and the developing reader is consigned largely to the medium of print by his well-meaning teachers.[6]

The view that picture books are only for babies and very young children is, of course, to see illustrations merely as a prop for the incompetent, rather than as an integral part of the work as a whole, or an extension and development of it. This is a bit odd, since no one as far as I know refuses to watch television or see a film on the grounds that the pictures are unnecessary or add little to the narrative! But in literature words sometimes seem to take on an almost sacred status, and nothing must be allowed to come between the reader and the pure unadulterated text. In fact, of course, nothing is lost and much can be gained by reading picture books as well as (not instead of) other types of literature. Picture books, in other words, do not compete with traditional novels and stories for older children, but complement them perfectly. And there are plenty of really good examples of picture books for older children to choose from, as Elaine Moss has demonstrated with her very useful guide.[7]

Charles Keeping's illustrated version of Alfred Noyes' *The Highwayman* was published in 1981 by Oxford University Press. As is well known, the poem describes how a highwayman returns to his lover who has been taken hostage by King George's men. She fires a musket, successfully warning him of the danger, but killing herself at the same time. Later the highwayman returns for revenge but is himself shot down. At the end of the poem, however, a ghostly highwayman comes back to be reunited with his lover.

The poem is written in a wonderful melodramatic style; not great poetry perhaps, but absolutely appropriate to such an emotional and romantic story of love and death:

Her eyes grew wide for a moment; she drew one last deep breath,
Then her finger moved in the moonlight,
  Her musket shattered the moonlight,
Shattered her breast in the moonlight and warned him − with her death.

Unlike the books discussed previously, Keeping's illustrations are in monochrome. But somehow one hardly notices because the range of shades of light and dark is so wide and varied. All the pictures are superbly drawn, but in particular the faces and gestures of the characters, whether in loving glance or in the agony of betrayal, are extraordinarily powerful. In all, the book provides a most memorable experience: the pictures heighten and deepen the meaning of the poem, without overwhelming the text.

Until now I have mainly tried to emphasize the value of picture books for aspects of children's language development, since probably for most teachers this is their most important function. However, I hope it has also become clear that picture books can have wider implications for children's learning. In the case of *The Highwayman*, not only can the reader look at the work of a gifted artist at the height of his powers, but the book also opens up for consideration and discussion some important moral and emotional themes: love and hatred; betrayal and self-sacrifice; revenge and forgiveness. Powerful stuff, but ideal for adolescent readers!

Picture Books, Readers and Learners

At this point we consider more directly one of the questions at the beginning of the chapter, in the light of the previous discussion. What is unique about picture

Back, he spurred like a madman, shouting a curse to the sky,
With the white road smoking behind him and his rapier brandished high
Blood-red were his spurs i' the golden noon; wine-red was his velvet
    coat;

Reprinted from *The Highwayman* by Alfred Noyes, 1981, illustrated by Charles Keeping,
© Charles Keeping (1981).

books? What can pictures do that text alone cannot, or what do they do in quite a
different way? It may be useful to consider briefly some of the ways in which
different kinds of picture book work, although these categories are not clear cut
in practice because most picture books fulfil more than one function.

Firstly, in wordless books where the pictures in a sense substitute words, a complete experience is provided without any need for text. Actually, of course, 'wordless' is something of a misnomer since such books demand that the reader provides the words him or herself, which is a highly complex activity requiring sophisticated linguistic skills. The fact that even very young children can learn to do this easily and apparently effortlessly is quite remarkable. Also, as in the example of *Sunshine*, not only is the experience of reading such books valuable in terms of children's language development, but it also has important implications for teaching children how pictures are made and how they work, and how they can respond appropriately to visual material.

In a second type of picture book, the pictures provide similar, but never identical, information to that of the text. In very different ways, some of the pictures in both *The Jolly Postman* and *The Highwayman* are of this kind, providing support and encouragement for the inexperienced or unsophisticated reader. But in good picture books like these they do much more as well: they entertain, stimulate and challenge the reader, greatly extending the range of meanings carried by the text.

Thirdly, as in picture books like *Rosie's Walk* and *Come Away from the Water, Shirley*, the pictures modify, contrast or even contradict what is said in the text. In many of the very best picture books one of the most significant (and enjoyable) tasks for the reader is to resolve the ambiguity or tension between the two, to fill the gap between words and pictures.

In each case, then, illustrations do not only provide support for children learning to read or developing their reading competencies; nor are they merely decorative. They also require intellectual work of other kinds: the reader is invited to construct his or her own meanings from the experience provided by text and pictures working together interdependently. In addition, good picture books also provide a range of visual experience which can extend and develop children's artistic tastes. Just as the written story can provide a meaningful literary experience as well as material with which to learn and practise skills, so the pictures can provoke a significant response at the same time as teaching children the conventions of visual representation. By looking at a picture book by Jan Ormerod, Pat Hutchins, John Burningham, the Ahlbergs, Charles Keeping or many others, children are encountering the work of highly talented and skilful artists. Through such encounters children can increasingly learn to respond to good quality artistic as well as literary material.

Conclusion

Finally, and at the risk of repeating what has been said earlier, it may be worth summarizing briefly what the picture books discussed in this chapter have in common, in spite of their differences in style, tone and theme. It may be helpful to bear in mind these characteristics of good picture books when criteria for the choice of particular texts for classroom use are discussed in more detail in Chapter 3. However, while these particular picture books are certainly good examples of the genre, they are not at all unique or untypical of the very high standards of text and illustration that are now available. There are hundreds more excellent books to which the following could be applied:

- They are physically well produced and attractively printed and bound.
- The text is well written, and the language is appropriate to the theme.
- The pictures are of high quality, and are appropriate to the theme.
- The text and illustrations are dynamically related: they work together interdependently.
- Both words and pictures require intellectual work by the reader; they invite the reader to construct meaning.
- They can be read and appreciated by readers of varied maturity and reading competence; most are accessible at some level to readers who lack fluency and/or sophistication.
- The stories are meaningful and coherent, and are inherently entertaining, interesting and satisfying.
- They provide opportunities for learning the techniques and conventions of visual representation, and for learning to appreciate artistic work.
- They provide opportunity for learning and practising the skills of language and reading, and for acquiring new ones.
- They directly or indirectly relate to real experience and/or real feelings.
- They invite sharing and co-operative work.
- They provide opportunities for discussion and other follow-up activities.

Notes and References

1. Opie, I. and P., *The Lore and Language of Schoolchildren*, Oxford University Press, 1959/London, Paladin, 1977; *Children's Games in Street and Playground*, Oxford University Press, 1984.

2. For an interesting discussion of these conventions, see also Spink, J., *Children as Readers*, London, Clive Bingley, 1989, chapter 5.

3. Meek, M., *How Texts Teach What Readers Learn*, Stroud, Thimble Press, 1988.

4. Benton, M. and Fox, G., *Teaching Literature Nine to Fourteen*, Oxford University Press, 1985.

5. Department of Education and Science/Welsh Office, *English For Ages 5 to 11*, London, National Curriculum Council, 1988.

6. Benton and Fox, *op. cit.*, p. 70.

7. Moss, E., *Picture Books for Young People 9–13* (2nd edn), Stroud, Thimble Press, 1988.

Picture Books Mentioned in the Text

Ahlberg, J. and A., *The Jolly Postman*, Heinemann.
Burningham, J., *Come Away from the Water, Shirley*, Cape/Picture Lion.
Hutchins, P., *Rosie's Walk*, Bodley Head/Picture Puffin.
Keeping, C., *The Highwayman*, Oxford University Press.
Ormerod, J., *Sunshine*, Picture Puffin.
Ormerod, J., *Moonlight*, Viking Kestrel/Picture Puffin.

3
CHOOSING PICTURE BOOKS

One implication of the preceding chapters is that a crucial role of the teacher is to encourage, but not force, children to read. But what material should we use? What should we encourage the children to read? The answer at first, I suggest, is almost anything. Before we even start thinking about the quality of the material we provide for children, the first essential is for children to turn naturally to the written word, of any kind, for enjoyment. I suggested earlier, in relation to the reluctance of some teachers to make use of picture books with older children, that it is sometimes implied that a central function of the teacher of language and literature is to introduce children to literary material of the very highest quality, and that therefore children should be weaned away from dependence on illustrations as fast as possible. Personally, I would not wish to dispute the first part of this as an aim for the very long term (even though what counts as the highest quality for young people is often far from obvious). But in the primary school it is much more important that children's enthusiasm for reading is developed and maintained, and that teachers do not turn children off by force-feeding them with material which is conceptually and linguistically very sophisticated. *The Merchant of Venice* is a very fine play, but not for the ten year olds whom I recently saw reading it as a class text!

Only when and if children are in fact reading something is it appropriate to be greatly concerned about encouraging them to read better quality material. As Peter Dickinson has plausibly argued,[1] even reading matter which to an adult's eye has no visible aesthetic or educational value may have a part to play in children's literary experience. It may be, then, that even if we cannot bring ourselves positively to encourage children to read comics, pulp dot-to-dot books or the most banal television spin-offs, we should not be too critical of their enthusiasm for such material. Better reading rubbish, perhaps, than reading nothing! Only at the point when children are motivated to turn to the written word with enthusiasm is it worth considering criteria which may enable teachers, and increasingly the children themselves, to discriminate between the excellent and the second rate, and between the second rate and the awful.

With this caution in mind, then, on what basis can the teacher choose, and help children to choose, picture books which first and foremost children will enjoy, but which will also enable them to develop further their literary (and other) competencies? Perhaps there are nine criteria which teachers may find useful to consider.

Physical Characteristics

There are first of all some straightforward matters of the physical characteristics of books. For classroom use, books must be reasonably robust. There are some delightful pop-up and lift-the-flap books in particular which are both expensive and very fragile. It may be that these are not suitable for general classroom use, although a copy to be used by the teacher with a group may be worthwhile. In general, hardback books are much longer lasting, but of course you get fewer books for your money, and finances are always tight in primary schools. It may be that a mixture of hardbacks, for those titles which are reasonably certain to be particularly popular with the children, plus a range of paperbacks would be the best strategy. The paper should be of good quality, and the pages in the book must be firmly attached, whether sewn or stapled — it sounds too obvious to mention, but there are plenty of books that seem to fall apart when you so much as glance at them! Books with laminated plastic covers are also to be preferred, since ordinary dust jackets become very tatty. Some firms[2] supply selections of books for different ages of children ready covered, or alternatively plastic covers can be purchased separately. Picture books vary greatly in size and are often physically bigger than other books; normally this does not cause too much difficulty unless the books are very large, in which case storage problems may arise.

Illustrations

Picture books must be visually attractive; in particular there is evidence[3] that the front cover is absolutely crucial. It is largely the front cover picture that answers the question, 'Do I think this one will be worth reading?' that children ask themselves when picking up a book or seeing it on display.

The pictures within the book must be aesthetically pleasing to children (not necessarily to adults). This is not always easy to judge because it is not always obvious what pictures children will find attractive, and of course individuals differ in their preferences; nor is available research much help.[4] The best policy may well be to try different books with different children, and learn by experience. Generally, however, it does seem that the younger the children the more the pictures need to be clear, bold, bright and uncluttered. It is worth bearing in mind that there are many picture books with illustrations that adults think are wonderful (such books sometimes win literary prizes) but few children like.

Most modern picture books are in full colour, but this is not always essential. Arnold Lobel uses only subdued browns and greens in his excellent *Frog and Toad* books, for example, and much of Charles Keeping's work is in shades of black and brown, but both are very effective.

The text should be at least large enough to be clear, and it should not be printed over the illustrations because such text is much more difficult to read. The words should be arranged appropriately in relation to the illustrations. Some authors (such as Helen Nicoll and Jan Pienkowski in their *Meg and Mog* series) have used text in particularly innovative and attractive ways, and children often find such books irresistible.

Language

Very significant criteria relate to the language of the book: clearly, picture books should use language which is appropriate and natural to the theme, and which enables children to anticipate and predict with reasonable expectation of success. It may be useful, as Liz Waterland suggests, for teachers to ask themselves as they look at a book whether the story is one which can be read aloud by adults in a natural voice, and without sounding forced. 'Is the language natural, predictable, "sensible" and meaningful?', she asks.[5] Is the book, in other words, linguistically alive? Is the story imaginatively worthwhile, and is the language sensitive and appropriate?

There should also perhaps be some consistency in the relationship between, on the one hand, the grammar, syntax and vocabulary of the text and, on the other, the interest level of the story as a whole. There are some books whose topic would interest a five or six year old, yet which are written using a complex or highly metaphorical language that is beyond the capacity of children to read, and in extreme cases even to understand. What, for example, would a young child make of: 'As dawn stole in, his eyes fell upon the floor'?[6] The *Gumdrop* books by Val Biro, for example, excellent though they are in many ways, are difficult reading considering that the stories generally appeal to children between five and eight or so. If an adult is using such books with children, he or she can explain and clarify where necessary, but the books would be a struggle for most young children reading on their own. This is not, of course, to say that the vocabulary or construction of the story must be entirely accessible given the child's existing abilities, since we do want children to make progress through increasingly challenging material. But for any individual there is clearly a limit to the degree of syntactical or grammatical complexity with which he or she can reasonably be expected to cope.

Range

By range I mean that we should try to provide a variety of both text and illustration to encourage children to reach out beyond the boundaries of what they feel comfortable with at any one time. This does not necessarily mean providing books which are more difficult to read or which contain more sophisticated pictures (although it may do), but it does mean giving children as wide a range of experiences as possible. It is clearly of great value to provide texts which have different contexts, themes, vocabularies, rhythms, styles and tones. Then young children can begin to appreciate the variety of purposes and effects of different authors writing in very different ways. This is fairly obvious; but what is perhaps less obvious to teachers is the importance of giving children a similar variety of experience in looking at different types of picture. Some examples may make the point: children should see the superb artistry of Charles Keeping's illustrations for *Beowulf* as well as the busy domesticity of much of the Ahlbergs' work; they should have the opportunity to enjoy the anarchic wit of Quentin Blake or Babette Cole and the glowing colours of Brian Wildsmith and Errol Le Cain; they should experience the bizarre surrealism of Anthony Browne's pictures as well as the sweeping panoramas of Philippe Dupasquier's illustrations in *Going West*; and they should look at the inspired pictures (and words) of Jan Pienkowski's *Christmas* as well as the beautifully executed watercolours of Michael Foreman.

Children respond to different pictures and texts in ways as varied as their responses to any other experience: from unqualified enthusiasm to outright rejection, or anything in between. The point is not to impose a model of what is best, or approved, but to expose children to a wide range of material, so that they can begin to develop their own tastes and their own criteria for choice.

Readability

Given that there are hundreds of good books available, further criteria may be needed which enable teachers to single out just a few as being worth reading and worth making available to children. Waterland's criteria are again helpful in distinguishing those books which are mediocre from those which are really outstanding. Is the book, she asks, multi-layered? That is, can it be enjoyed by child readers of different attainments, including virtual non-readers, and by adults too? A really good picture book is one that can provide an enjoyable experience at a variety of levels. And does the book have attributes that will attract children, such as humour, rhythm, familiarity, colour? Humour is a particularly important criterion as far as children are concerned, especially humour which shares a joke between author and reader (and not where the adult writer is having a joke at the child's expense). Further, do the text and the illustrations work together so as to create an experience which in a sense is greater than the sum of its parts, a meaningful whole? Or is the text so dominant that the illustrations are really unnecessary? Finally, and perhaps most significant of all, says Waterland, is the book real, written by an author with a story to tell? Or is it just a book produced to a formula or to the requirements of the publisher of a reading scheme? It may be that, with the recent publication of new and attractive reading schemes such as E.J. Arnold's 'Story Chest', Oxford University Press's 'Reading Tree' and Longman's 'Reading World', all of which incorporate a variety of well-written and illustrated stories and story books, the distinction that Waterland makes between schemes (bad) and 'real books' (good) is less clear cut than she asserts. Nevertheless, the basic point that the story is more important than a controlled vocabulary, or endless repetition of a few words or phrases, is surely valid.

Individual Preferences

Waterland's criteria are quite reasonably aimed at teachers, but in an important sense no one can really act as final arbiter of the value of a book except the child him or herself. An important criterion is thus what might be called 'taste it and choose' or 'suck it and see'! Children are individuals with often idiosyncratic tastes and interests. Excellent books do not necessarily appeal to all children to the same extent, or indeed at all. Why should they? After all, adults are at least as varied in their reading preferences. And children's interests change and develop over time − even from day to day it sometimes seems! As a starting point, teachers might wish to find out what kinds of book children like, by asking them to reply orally or in writing to a few simple questions: for example, what is the best book you have ever read? are there any books you have read more than once? what book are you reading at the moment? The answers to such questions can provide an initial basis for the teacher's decision making. Obviously as the teacher develops an increasingly intimate knowledge of the children in the class, he or she can begin to adapt what is provided to the known interests and enthusiasms of the children, and take further account of their reactions to the books they read.

This process of interaction between child and teacher is very productive, provided it is genuine and not in reality rigid teacher control of pupil choices thinly disguised. Sometimes the teacher may not even be aware that he or she is exerting such control; it often takes a conscious effort not to do so. In one school I taught in, a large proportion of the non-fiction books in the school library were about yachts and sailing. It just so happened that the headteacher, who ordered all the books for the school, had a consuming passion for anything that floated! If, however, the teacher can genuinely and openly discuss, consult and take seriously children's preferences, then children may more readily develop positive attitudes towards books because they are reading material which they enjoy, which is at approximately the right cognitive and emotional level, and which they have played some part in selecting. And the process is of benefit to teachers too: they can extend their knowledge of books, of the children, and of the ways books and children interact. Peggy Heeks puts it very sensibly:

> Reading advice begins with getting to know the reader, finding out what he already likes, accepting his current enthusiasms, and taking care not to demolish these through one's own perception of literary quality ... what our counselling should reinforce in this early stage is the primacy of pleasure. Let us observe the features which children most enjoy, the humour, the domestic links, the tall stories, the rhythms and visual enjoyments, and make sure these satisfactions are available in the books we introduce.[7]

Gender, Race, Class

In the last ten or fifteen years, teachers have become much more conscious of the social attitudes and values that books incorporate, in particular in relation to ethnicity, social class, gender, disability, aspects of the environment and so on. Several writers[8] have pointed to the racial stereotypes implicit in some books for young children: the images of Afro-Caribbean or Asian people as strange, as peculiar, even as inferior. Other authors[9] have argued that much of children's literature is damagingly middle class in its assumptions and values, and that it distorts and misrepresents, or even excludes altogether, the experience of ordinary working people. The models of gender that are often portrayed in children's books have also been much criticized:[10] Mum endlessly tied to domestic routine while Dad goes out to work; boys taking leadership roles in the story while girls tag along behind, and so on.

Recently authors and publishers of children's books have become more aware of such issues, and many excellent books are now available which portray realistically and sensitively members of various ethnic, racial and social class groups, the roles of girls and women in society, and other important issues (some of these books are reviewed in Chapters 8 to 11). But highly offensive material can still be found in schools: several of the books in the popular Ladybird Key Words Reading Scheme treat gender-roles in ways that can only be described as unrealistic and insulting, and books like the ghastly *Story of Little Black Sambo* remain in print so presumably someone still buys them. Amazingly, there is even a book produced as recently as 1984 which advocates the use of this material in classrooms.[11] This may be an extreme case, but the social and racial attitudes implicit (and sometimes explicit) in the work of popular authors like Enid Blyton, Hugh Lofting and W.E. Johns among many others have also been criticized as quite inappropriate for an increasingly diverse and pluralist society like ours.[12]

Children's basic social attitudes begin to take shape in their very early years, and it really is unacceptable for teachers to ignore such issues on the grounds that they are too complex for young children to understand; to do so is to abandon children to the morality of the peer group and the mass media. Teachers have a significant role to play in presenting even the youngest children with appropriate models of attitude and behaviour, and so it seems perverse to provide reading material which is very seriously flawed when there is much that is positive and thoughtful available.[13]

These comments may appear to conflict with what was said earlier about being concerned first and foremost with children reading anything at all as long as they are reading. What if the book they really want to read is *Little Black Sambo* or something similar? This is not an easy question to answer, and leads into fundamental questions of censorship, about which opinions differ sharply. Some teachers feel that a good way of handling such material is to use it deliberately in the classroom, to raise issues of sexism and racism head on, as it were. By discussion and analysis such reading may help children to become critical readers, capable of viewing texts in their historical and social context. This seems to me an admirable idea, but one which takes very skilled teaching to accomplish, especially with young children. I would not myself encourage children to read such books, and indeed would do my best to help them to find something better (and more enjoyable); nor would I make books available in the classroom that I thought were morally repugnant. But I have never actually removed a book from a child; nor, in spite of frequent temptation, would I want to do so.

Morality and Didacticism

A complementary issue, and one that is equally difficult to come to grips with, is that of didacticism. Of course, most if not all picture books imply aspects of morality: kindness, taking care and being truthful are some of the most common. As Harold Rosen has asserted, all stories 'carry in their sub-text affirmations of what it means to be a proper person and what constitutes proper behaviour'.[14] It may be that most such books can be regarded as positive and useful because they are also good stories in their own right. A rule of thumb might therefore be that a good picture book ought to have both artistic *and* moral qualities. There are some books which would fail such a test because, although they are well written, they have morally repugnant implications (like *Little Black Sambo*). More frequently, books would fail because their ethical precepts, despite being widely acceptable, are both very explicit and in a sense

almost forced on the reader; the story is relegated to being merely the vehicl
moralizing of one kind or another. The case quoted by Heeks of 'a nineteenth
century Puss in Boots calling for milk at the King's court with the explanation
that "on principle he was a teetotaller"'[15] may seem merely amusing now, but
there are plenty of modern examples too. Take, for instance, Oralee Wachter's
No More Secrets For Me, published in 1986 by Puffin, whose central theme is
how children can avoid sexual abuse. This is a very important theme, and it is
admittedly extremely difficult to write in a way that is helpful to a child who has
problems, without being so specific as to frighten and bewilder children who
have not. Yet the four stories in the book are really not stories at all; they are dull
and didactic, thinly veiled propaganda (compare the books on similar themes by
Althea and by Helen Hollick discussed in Chapter 10). My own view is that
themes of this kind do need to be tackled, but either in carefully written
information books or by skilled authors who can raise such issues in the context
of stories that are alive and dynamic in their own right. For example, in the work
of Michael Foreman (see Chapter 11) themes such as world hunger, pollution
and race relations are dealt with in ways that young children can understand and
appreciate, yet without giving one the feeling of being preached at. In such
books the message is certainly powerful and compelling, but also an integral part
of a literary and artistic whole. Even work of undoubted quality, however, may
need to be introduced with care: books like John Burningham's *Granpa* and
Susan Varley's *Badger's Parting Gifts*, for example, are beautifully judged
picture books which could help a child to come to terms with the death of a
relative, but they would need to be handled sensitively by the teacher.

While the difference between the most blatantly didactic books and those
which imply moral attitudes by tremendous imaginative power is fairly easy to
spot, unfortunately in practice most books are not so readily categorized: many
books fall into a grey area where it is hard to make such clear-cut distinctions. It
may be that, in all but the most extreme cases, teachers would wish to give the
book the benefit of the doubt, but at least teachers need to have considered the
issue and taken a positive decision.

Relevance

Relevance, finally, is another very tricky concept. It has sometimes been used to
assert that children who live in particular social circumstances should be
provided with books which directly reflect those conditions. Thus, for example,
it has been suggested that children who live in working-class areas of inner cities
should hear and read stories about doing the pools, eating fish and chips, playing
in the street and so on. There is, of course, nothing wrong in principle with such
themes, provided that the idea of relevance is not used to limit children's reading

experience to such material. The concept of relevance should include the emotional as well as the social, and stories about dragons or princesses or elephants or other topics beyond children's immediate experience may thus be as relevant as stories set in streets and playgrounds. After all, few of us as adults are ever likely to be in Hamlet's predicament, yet we may find the play relevant to us in other than the physical and literal senses. As primary teachers we should, then, be concerned to' ensure that children read and hear stories that have the potential to enlarge their understanding of themselves, their relationships and their social world, not just to reflect the conditions and contexts in which they live.

Conclusion

It may be useful to conclude with a simple summary list of questions which teachers may wish to ask themselves in order to construct criteria for choice of picture books:

- Is the book physically well produced?
- Is the story coherent, imaginative and interesting?
- Is the book well written? Does it read aloud well?
- Is the language accessible and appropriate?
- Are the illustrations attractive and appropriate?
- Are words and pictures interdependent?
- Is the book relevant to children's interests?
- Are the book's moral implications acceptable?
- Does the book treat race, gender and social class positively?
- Is the book overall enjoyable and worthwhile?

If picture books are as valuable as has been suggested, then one might expect them to be in constant use in every classroom. In fact this does not always seem to be the case. One recent survey of the use of fiction in classrooms, based on questionnaire responses from teachers in some four hundred schools,[16] concluded that many teachers of infant classes used only reading schemes or associated material, presumably on the assumption that these constituted a sufficient and adequate reading diet. Particularly notable was the absence of picture book titles from the books that the teachers most often listed as being in use, and in fact no individual picture book or series of books came anywhere near general popularity.

There are probably many reasons for this apparent neglect of picture books, but one may be some teachers' uncertainty about how actually to make use of them in the classroom. If so, it is important to suggest ways in which picture books can be used, which is the main concern of the next three chapters.

Notes and References

1. Dickinson, P., 'A defence of rubbish', *Children's Literature in Education*, no. 3, 1970.

2. Such as Kaleidoscope, Books for Students, Bird Road, Heathcote, Warwick CV34 6TB. Various age- and attainment-related selections of paperbacks are offered, each costing the total retail price of all the books included. These come with free plastic covers, storage boxes and notes for teachers. Such pre-selected boxes of books are useful for the busy teacher, but obviously are unlikely to match exactly the interests and reading competence of any particular class of children.

3. Lake, W., 'Never the twain shall meet: reading interests and gender', in Marriott, S. *et al.*, *More Words*, Coleraine, New University of Ulster, 1984.

4. For a critical summary, see Berridge, C., 'Illustrators, books, and children: an illustrator's viewpoint', *Children's Literature in Education*, no. 11, 1980. See also Adams F., *Children's Preferences in Picture Book Illustration*, Glasgow, Jordanhill College, 1977, Hughes, S., 'Word and image', in Fearn, M. (ed.), *Only the Best is Good Enough*, London, Rossendale, 1985.

5. Waterland, L., *Read With Me* (2nd edn), Stroud, Thimble Press, 1988, p. 46.

6. Quoted by Donaldson, M., 'Literature and language development', in Hoffman, M. *et al.* (eds.), *Children, Language and Literature*, Milton Keynes, Open University Press, 1982.

7. Heeks, P., *Choosing and Using Books in the First School*, London, Macmillan, 1981, p. 120.

8. Such as Klein, G., *Reading into Racism*, London, Routledge & Kegan Paul, 1985.

9. See Leeson, R., *Children's Books and Class Society*, London, Writers and Readers Publishing Co-operative, 1977; Leeson, R., *Reading and Righting*, London, Collins, 1985.

10. See, for example, Zimet, S.G., *Print and Prejudice*, London, Hodder & Stoughton, 1976; Children's Rights Workshop, *Sexism in Children's Books*, London, Writers and Readers Publishing Co-operative, 1976.

11. Cass, J.E., *Literature and the Young Child* (2nd edn), Harlow, Longman, 1984.

12. See Dixon, B., *Catching Them Young: Vol. 1 Sex Race and Class in Children's Fiction*; *Vol. 2 Political Ideas in Children's Fiction*, London, Pluto, 1977.

13. For some practical suggestions, see Smidt, S., 'Reading and our multi-cultural society', in Moon, C. (ed.), *Practical Ways to Teach Reading*, London, Ward Lock, 1985.

14. Quoted by Meek, M. and Mills, C., 'The open space', in Meek, M. and Mills, C. (eds.), *Language and Literacy in the Primary School*, Lewes, Falmer Press, 1988. See also Williams, G., 'Naive and serious questions: the role of text criticism in primary education' in the same volume.

15. Heeks, *op. cit.*, p. 71.

16. Marriott, S., 'Teachers' use of fiction in primary schools in Northern Ireland', *Irish Journal of Education*, Vol. 20, 1986.

Picture Books Mentioned in the Text

Biro, V., Gumdrop series, Picture Puffin.
Burningham, J., *Granpa*, Cape/Picture Puffin.
Keeping, C., *Beowulf*, Oxford University Press.

Lobel, A., Frog and Toad series, World's Work/Young Puffin.
Nicoll, H. and Pienkowski, J., Meg and Mog series, Heinemann/Picture Puffin.
Pienkowski, J., *Christmas*, Heinemann/Picture Puffin.
Varley, S., *Badger's Parting Gifts*, Andersen/Picture Lion.
Wachter, O., *No More Secrets For Me*, Puffin.
Waddell, M., *Going West*, Andersen/Picture Puffin.

4
USING PICTURE BOOKS: THE HOME AND THE SCHOOL

Teachers have probably always recognized to some degree the importance of parents in the educational process, but in recent years the part they have to play has become even more apparent. For example, recent legislation has given the opinions and ideas of parents, mediated through governing bodies, a significant role in the life of schools.

A vast literature has grown up on the subject of parental involvement in education,[1] and parents are increasingly coming to be seen as partners of teachers, with rather different but equally valuable roles to play, especially in the early years of schooling.

Parents and Children before School

Obviously parents have a fundamental educative role before school starts, and this is particularly true in the case of children's language development. The process of acquisition and development of language does not begin at the age of four or five; nor does it only occur after nine o'clock on Monday to Friday mornings! Rather, it begins at birth and continues unceasingly thereafter. And not only oral language; the foundations of literacy are laid in the pre-school years. Very tiny babies enjoy the colour and pattern of picture books, the sound of talk and the physical experience of being held comfortably in Mum or Dad's arms. Such early experience is certainly worthwhile in terms of introducing children to the pleasure to be found in books, but it is also very significant for learning to read in school. As Dorothy Butler has suggested in her very useful book:

> A baby is learning about the way language arises from the page each time his parent opens a book, from earliest days. He is linking the human voice to the print at a very early age. Given repeated opportunity, he notices how the adult attends to the black marks, how he can't go on reading if the page is turned too soon ...[2]

It is certainly possible for children to come to school already enthusiastic about books and reading; it is also, of course, possible for them to arrive doubtful about reading and all it entails, if not positively antagonistic. Parents (and play-group leaders, nursery teachers, aunties, uncles, baby-sitters and all the other adults with whom a child comes into contact) have therefore an absolutely central role, a role which continues in modified forms all through the primary school years.

Here is an example of what children can achieve through parental interest and involvement, allied to a stimulating picture book. It is an extract from the transcript of a tape recording. The child, aged three and a half, is 'reading' Roger Hargreaves' *Mr Impossible*. Also present are Mum, Dad and older brother (aged five and a half), although the following is continuous speech by the younger child apart from one brief interjection which has been omitted. The italicized section refers to the text and picture reprinted on p. 43.

> Child: Mr Impossible can fly over house − can jump over house − that's impossible! Mr Impossible can make himself invisible − all that he had to do [cough] is sit − is stand up and think about it being invisible and then he became invisible. That's impossible! Mr Impossible can fly − all that he had to do was flap his hands about − about and then he went up in the air. That's impossible! Now once Mr − oh! Mr Impossible had his house in a very impossible place − it's up in a tree! [laughter] − Well once Mr Impossible met a boy called William − hello said William hello said Mr Impossible − [interjection]. *Can you climb up that tree said Willi − can you do things impossible? Yes said Mr Impossible [laughter]. Can you climb up that tree? I can do better than that [cough]. I can walk up that tree − and he did [laughter]* ...

This child cannot decode any print at all. He is in fact 'reading' by remembering the story from the occasion he has heard it read to him by Mum, and, most importantly, by using the cues provided by the illustrations. Clearly the pictures are crucial here: they provide the child with a framework within which he can construct his own version of the story. And thus, at the age of three and a half, he is able to do several difficult tasks which are fundamental to skilled reading. He can create meaning from a text by engaging in a kind of dialogue with the author, and he can sustain the narrative thread through a long (seventeen double-page spreads) and quite complex book. He has acquired not only a clear understanding of what stories are and how they work, but also the confidence to incorporate that understanding into his own production. He has already grasped so much of what reading is and what makes a story work, before he ever goes near a school or a teacher. The knowledge, understanding and confidence that he has acquired has surely come from a combination of parental involvement and enthusiasm for books and stories, and also from the support and structure provided by the nature of the picture

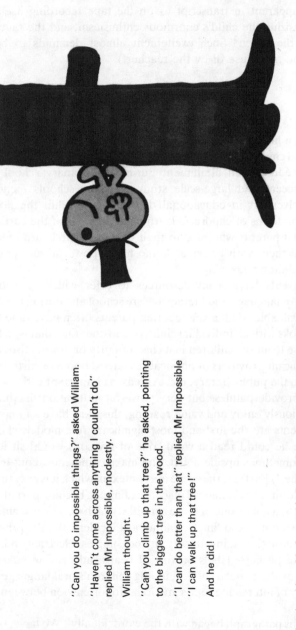

"Can you do impossible things?" asked William.

"Haven't come across anything I couldn't do" replied Mr Impossible, modestly.

William thought.

"Can you climb up that tree?" he asked, pointing to the biggest tree in the wood.

"I can do better than that" replied Mr Impossible "I can walk up that tree!"

And he did!

book itself; a very clear demonstration of the way in which words and pictures can be related in early reading experiences. (Although unfortunately it is not so apparent in transcript as on the tape recording itself, it is also worth emphasizing the child's enormous enthusiasm, and the raucous delight he takes in the story.[3] Such excitement almost demands to be fostered, developed and made use of by the teacher!)

Parents and Children at School

If this example shows anecdotally what parents and other adults can do to give children a head start in terms of reading long before they go to school, parental involvement has also been shown by researchers to be of significance in children's educational attainment during the primary school years. For example, a recent and large-scale study of junior schools[4] concluded that parental involvement in educational development within the home was of great benefit in terms of children's learning in all areas of the curriculum, and specifically that parents who read to their children, who heard them read and who provided them with books at home had a powerful and positive effect upon their children's learning.

Ideally, parents have many resources to offer which contribute to the development of language and literacy before school and during the early school years. Most valuable of all is the fact that parents often have time to read and talk about books with an individual child, one to one, time that is so hard for the teacher to give to all the children in a class of thirty or more. Also, parents can become significant providers of physical resources: books as birthday presents, family trips to the public library, etc. At least as important is the way in which parents can provide painless but very powerful motivation: if Mum and Dad read and obviously enjoy and value reading, this must have an impact on their children; parents are the first and most significant role models children have. (Long before he could read a word, one of my sons would sit looking at a newspaper, sometimes upside down, and make comments about it to his even younger brother!) Further, the home is a context in which it is easy for books and reading to take an entirely natural place; reading can become part of the family's everyday life, and not be one of those activities which only ever seems to be done in school classrooms. And finally, and almost incidentally, the printed word in the broadest sense (including nursery rhymes, jingles, electricity bills, shopping lists, cornflake packets, labels on tins of beans, advertising hoardings, road signs, etc.) provides a means of developing children's oral language through an endless supply of interesting topics and ideas for discussion between parent and child.

The previous paragraph began with the word 'ideally'! We have, of course, to recognize that such circumstances and outcomes do not always occur unless efforts are made by teachers. In some cases parents are unwilling or unable to help; more often, perhaps, they want to do anything and everything to support their children's progress, but need guidance to make their efforts fully productive.

Within the framework of whatever home—school liaison policy exists in the school, and assuming that parent—teacher relationships are generally reasonably open and supportive there is much that the teacher of young children can do to encourage and assist parents. Not all the following suggestions will be relevant to every situation, but some of them may be helpful.

First of all, perhaps, parents should hear and understand the message loud and clear that parents, teachers and children are partners in the educational process. It is therefore no longer the case, if it ever was, that parents should be encouraged to regard the teaching of literacy (or almost anything else, for that matter) as exclusively a matter for the professionals; both parents and teachers have vital educational roles which overlap to some extent, but are obviously not identical. Thus any formal or informal means which involve parents in literacy-related activities with their children of school age or even younger should be encouraged and welcomed. They need to be developed and enhanced by the teacher, but the first stage is to ensure that parents are enabled to participate, are made to feel welcome.[5]

Some way of explaining to parents the school's and the teachers' approach to reading is absolutely essential. This can be achieved by means of booklets sent home, meetings, informal contacts, home visits, or a combination of strategies. Most parents are naturally keen that their children should quickly learn to read skilfully and fluently, and want to help the school to achieve this. They therefore deserve to have the teacher's approach explained clearly and simply (and frequently!). There is no reason to regard this as threatening to teachers' sense of professional expertise; rather, the more parents can be co-opted as allies, the better for the child's progress. If the school and the home are working at cross-purposes, a lot of avoidable difficulties may be created.

Whatever strategies and techniques are used, the emphasis on enjoyment is crucial. As Branston and Provis suggest,[6] this can be achieved by stressing to parents that the quality of the reading experience is more important than the quantity, that numbers of pages read is much less significant than the fact that children are motivated and excited by reading. It is clearly not helpful, for example, if parents communicate to their children such a desperate anxiety about reading progress that for the child reading becomes a tense and painful experience. (I have heard of cases where parents cover up the illustrations in a story to stop the child 'cheating' and to 'test' the child on the words; this is not a very constructive strategy, to put it mildly!)

Encouraging parents to read to their children at home, especially in the early stages, is vital. 'The golden rule for helping a child is still: read to him, and for him, in a way that will let him discover what reading is all about'.[7] Many families find that the regular bedtime story is a wonderful means of encouraging the reading habit among children (although the activity is, of course, valuable at any time of day). Teachers could recommend titles and/or authors particularly suitable for such purposes; Jim Trelease's *Read-Aloud Handbook*[8] provides much useful advice on this and many other aspects of story reading by parents.

Parents can also usefully listen to their children reading. In order to achieve a worthwhile experience for both parents and children, teachers may need both to supply attractive and appropriate books for children to take home, and also to explain to parents how the reading session can be made most productive. For example, it may be necessary to advise parents that to pressurize children into reading, or to make the child feel tense and anxious about his or her performance, is likely to be counter-productive. Further, it could be suggested that, if the child meets an unknown word while reading, the parent should supply it immediately, and not attempt to 'teach' it to the child (parents should not be encouraged to delve into the mysteries of phonics; that is one part of the teacher's job!). It may be best, at least initially, for the child to use books at home which he or she is familiar with and confident about. The teacher's emphasis should be on the fact that children who have pleasurable reading experiences are likely to learn to read more quickly and more effectively; anything which detracts from the children's enjoyment, and in particular attempts by parents formally to 'teach' reading strategies or techniques, should be avoided.

At the very least, in schools where a reading scheme book is routinely sent home, this could be supplemented or sometimes replaced by an appropriate picture book, and parents encouraged to read this with the child. It is worth remembering that the reading books taken home by the child convey a significant message to parents about the school's view of what reading is. The message implied by the Ahlbergs' *The Jolly Postman* is very different from that of *Ready to Read Book 9B* or some such title!

Picture books are suitable for home and school reading activities for many reasons, but perhaps particularly because they encourage talk, and the oral reconstruction of stories and ideas (as with *Mr Impossible*). A tremendous enrichment of oral language can arise out of discussion of the topics in picture books. Such discussion feeds back into an increased awareness of print in the environment, and an increased sophistication in children's choice of material to read and their critical awareness of its merits; and so the cyclical and interdependent process can continue indefinitely.

For these reasons, it is of great value to encourage parents to talk, and to provide opportunities for the children to talk, about the story and the pictures. Parents can be shown how the pictures can be used to provide cues, sustain the meanings of the text and construct a framework for the story. One possible strategy is for the teacher occasionally to make a tape recording of his or her own interaction with a child and a picture book; the tape can then be sent home so that parents can begin to learn something of the strategies the teacher uses. Alternatively, a simple form, or an ordinary exercise book, could be used for parents to record and comment on their child's reading activity at home, whether instigated by the school or not, which could be added to occasionally by the teacher's suggestions and advice ('Why don't you try ...?', 'Have you seen ...?', 'I'll send home a copy of ...', etc.).

In addition, parents could be encouraged to visit the school and read to or with individuals or groups of children in the classroom in a form of paired reading, for which again picture books are ideal.[9] If done systematically, this is valuable for both parents and children – and also for the teacher, who gains at least temporarily an extra pair of hands in the classroom! Some schools prefer parents not to help in classrooms in which their own children are taught, but others find that this causes no problems.

Parents can be advised, by the traditional note home, through informal contacts at the beginning and end of the school day, or by other means, of relevant local news such as public library membership information, availability of local bookshops, local events connected with the Book Week held annually in many areas, and so on.

Parents often become, more or less willingly, providers of books for children. It may therefore be useful to provide a list of suggestions of suitable and appropriate books, perhaps with a brief comment about each, that parents or other relations could buy for children at Christmas or on birthdays. Parents do not necessarily have a clear sense of what is appropriate for their children: a Mum I once knew bought a copy of *Black Beauty* as a Christmas present for her eleven-year-old but virtually non-reading son who was passionately interested in motorbikes. 'But he just won't sit down and read it', she said. I can't say I was surprised! Picture books make particularly attractive presents for young children, and so do the many books now published with an accompanying audio tape.[10]

A simple display of books in the corridor or the classroom can usefully attract parents' attention. And if children's work is displayed alongside the stories which stimulated it, the links between books and the work of the school is reinforced.

A number of commercial firms[11] offer relatively easily organized book clubs, whereby children are enabled to purchase books, including picture books, on a regular basis. The fact that children are buying and taking home books that they have chosen themselves and are really enthusiastic about is of obvious benefit, and, human nature being what it is, parents are likely to be particularly interested in books towards which they have made some financial commitment! And, of course, it may be possible for parents to play an active role in the organization and management of such clubs.

Parents could be encouraged to help children see the connections between televised children's stories (which are sometimes excellently done) and the books on which they are based; again such books may be available within the school or in the public library system.

A visit by the class to the local public library is enormously valuable, particularly if it is possible to involve parents as helpers. There is evidence[12] that the local library can be a highly significant stimulus of and resource for reading. Most librarians will be delighted to arrange a programme for children of any age, and while such visits are useful for all children, they are particularly valuable for those (and, if possible, their parents) who do not use the public library as part of their normal family routine; children can often be enrolled as members on the spot! Some schools undertake visits to the library as often as once a term by each class, and these visits are very worthwhile.

Finally, there are other rather more ambitious projects. Parent—teacher or similar association meetings could be set up which are devoted to introducing parents to children's books, perhaps with the assistance of the local public librarian. The organization and management of school bookshops requires time and skills that can very appropriately be provided by parents.[13] Parents could be invited to attend during visits by authors of picture books to the school or the local library. Some parents make excellent classroom storytellers. Branston and Provis's practical and helpful book[14] about the CAPER (Children and Parents Enjoying Reading) project provides many further detailed suggestions (and attractive photocopiable material) for the involvement of parents in the development of reading for pleasure and meaning. Not all teachers will want to take on the whole of the highly structured scheme that the authors describe, but many of their ideas are very useful indeed.

Conclusion

In this chapter I have tried to suggest that parents and teachers can and should work together, and that if they do the benefits to the children are enormous. However, from the teacher's point of view, using any of the suggestions I have made obviously necessitates spending time and energy, both of which may be in short supply given the enormous demands routinely placed on primary school teachers. Occasionally, too, attempting to build relationships with parents is not as easy and unproblematic a process as is sometimes implied, but proves to be complex, or confused or even tense. Nevertheless both research evidence and common sense suggest that parental involvement in literacy-related activities is likely to be of great value, and thus even small scale and very limited attempts by the teacher to develop a positive relationship with parents in this area are likely to be rewarding. And as teachers are well aware, the vast majority of parents are not obstreperous or difficult, but are desperately keen to help, and desperately nervous about doing the wrong thing. The more we can enable them to work with us, the better for the children.

Notes and References

1. See, for example, Craft, M. *et al.*, (eds.), *Linking Home and School*: A New Review (3rd. edn), London, Harper & Row, 1980; Tizard, B., Montimore, J. and Burchell, B., *Involving Parents in Nursery and Infants Schools: A Source Book for Teachers*, London, Grant McIntyre, 1981.

2. Butler, D., *Babies Need Books*, London, Bodley Head, 1980, p. 25.

3. Similar examples are provided in Beard, R., *Developing Reading 3–13*, London, Hodder & Stoughton, 1987, pp. 63–4; McKenzie, M., *Journeys into Literacy*, Huddersfield, Schofield & Sims, 1986, pp. 35–6.

4. Inner London Education Authority, *The Junior School Project: A Summary of the Main Findings*, London, ILEA, 1986.

5. See also Topping, K. and Wolfendale, S., (eds.), *Parental Involvement in Children's Reading*, London, Croom Helm, 1985.

6. Branston, P. and Provis, M., *Children and Parents Enjoying Reading*, London, Hodder & Stoughton, 1986, pp. 1–2.

7. Meek, M., *Learning to Read*, London, Bodley Head, 1982, p. 42.

8. Trelease, J., *The Read-Aloud Handbook*, Harmondsworth, Penguin, 1984.

9. For details see Reading and Language Information Centre, *Working Together: Parents, Teachers and Children*, University of Reading School of Education, 1987; Bloom, W., *Partnership with Parents in Reading*, Sevenoaks, Hodder & Stoughton, 1987.

10. See for example, those produced by Puffin Cover to Cover Storytapes. These are widely available, and also can be obtained by post from: Bags of Books, 7 South Street, Lewes, Sussex BN7 2BT. See also Redford, R., *Hear to Read*, available from the Book Trust, 45 East Hill, London SW18 2QZ.

11. Such as the Puffin Book Club, 27 Wrights Lane, London W8 5TZ, and several clubs run by Scholastic Publications Westfield Road, Southam, Leamington Spa, Warwickshire, CV33 0BR.

12. Clark, M., *Young Fluent Readers*, London, Heinemann, 1976.

13. See, for example, Noyes, D., 'Running a school bookshop', in Hoffman, M. *et al.* (eds.), *Children, Language and Literature*, Milton Keynes, Open University Press, 1982. See also Kennerley, P., *Running a School Bookshop*, London, Ward Lock, 1978. Advice is available from the School Bookshop Association, 1 Effingham Road, Lee, London SE12 8NZ.

14. Branston and Provis, *op. cit.*

Picture Books Mentioned in the Text

Ahlberg, J. and A., *The Jolly Postman*, Heinemann.
Hargreaves, R., *Mr Impossible*, Thurman Publishing.

5
USING PICTURE BOOKS: THE SCHOOL AND THE CLASSROOM

It is not difficult to use picture books in the classroom, but as with any other aspect of the curriculum much depends on the prior thinking and general preparation that the teacher has been able to devote to it. There are several desirable conditions for successful work, but of course classroom situations are often not ideal and any use is better than none (well, almost any!).

Picture Books in the Classroom

Context

The first requirement is that the teacher should be aware of the range and variety of picture books available, and have some developing sense of the appropriateness of different types of book for different children. This obviously involves some teacher reading and thus a certain amount of scarce time and energy, but on the other hand picture books are generally neither lengthy nor difficult to read, and in fact can often be enjoyed at an adult level. The reviews and other material in Chapters 7 to 11 are intended, among other purposes, to assist in the process of introducing teachers to new and worthwhile picture books.

The comments made earlier about parents' reading acting as a role model for children apply with equal force to teachers. If the teacher obviously reads and enjoys reading, this may well have greater long-term effect on children's progress than exhortations about the value of books and reading which the teacher does not appear to follow him or herself! This applies not only to children's books, of course: teachers can appropriately talk at some level with children about all kinds of leisure or everyday reading.

The physical conditions in which children and teachers work are important for a whole variety of reasons, but particularly in the context of reading picture books. Clearly, the creation of pleasant and comfortable surroundings is very difficult in some of the cramped and dilapidated conditions in which teachers and children have to work. But even a few cushions and an old piece of carpet in a corner marked off from the rest of the classroom by bookcases or cupboards adds something to the experience of picture books; somehow even such minimal concessions to comfort can change a routine school activity into something a bit special. The construction of more sophisticated book areas in the classroom is usefully discussed by Joan Dean.[1]

Resources

Enabling children to come into contact with more and better books is of course central, and thus availability is very important. There are still classrooms of very young children where no picture books can be found; there are many others where books are hidden away in stock cupboards or shelved in inaccessible libraries; let alone the regrettably common situation where the books are easily available but old, tatty and unappealing. The teacher I once met who was reluctant to let her pupils read the lovely new books available in her classroom on the grounds that 'the children tend to make the books dirty' may have been an extreme case, but it gives point to the assertion that books that are inaccessible for any reason are utterly useless. Picture books are only of value at the point when children are actively enabled to use them, even if this means, as it inevitably does, that books are eventually worn out. There is a fine line between encouraging children to take reasonable care of books, and being so concerned that children become almost afraid to touch them!

Teachers may wish to consider ways in which existing resources can be brought to children's attention more effectively and more frequently. For example, if there is a whole school collection, groups of children or the whole class could regularly visit to select books for temporary display and use in the classroom. In addition, it should be possible occasionally to make a simple but interesting classroom display on a seasonal theme or relating to a topic, which includes a few picture books alongside other relevant material. It is relatively easy to display picture books attractively, i.e. with the front cover rather than the spine visible, and if thought desirable to physically group a few books by theme (homes, colours, pirates, Christmas or whatever: see Appendix 2 pp. 133–40 for some suggestions). Teachers should take every opportunity to draw children's attention to such displays, but should also take care to vary the books so that what is easily accessible does not become so familiar that it is taken for granted. One teacher I know simply keeps a constantly changing selection of picture books on her desk for children to take to read in odd moments of the day, and somehow for the children this alone makes those books rather special. Another suggestion to draw older children's attention specifically to picture books, which otherwise might get lost among the shelves of fiction and non-fiction, is to to have a special shelf for 'Gold Star Picture Books',[2] each of which has, logically enough, a gold star on its spine.

Adding to existing resources is also often necessary, since books by their nature have a limited physical lifespan. Getting more and different books may of course cost money, which is frequently a scarce commodity in primary schools, and picture books, especially in hardback, are not cheap. There is something extra special about a brand new picture book which is often well worth the expense, but there are also ways of minimizing costs: second-hand bookshops (and even jumble sales) often have good quality children's books available very cheaply; children can be asked to donate titles they have grown out of, and are surprisingly often willing to do so; teachers can make productive use of their own family's unwanted books. But perhaps the best sources of all are the public library and the local schools library service, which will gladly lend selections of wonderful books, as well as providing much useful advice and expertise.

Classification

In some classrooms, library books are carefully colour coded by the teacher in terms of their reading difficulty. This has the obvious advantage of making it easier for children to select books which are at about the right level linguistically and conceptually. But there are disadvantages too: children's choice of books can become intensely and unproductively competitive ('I'm reading Blue books and you're still on those babyish Green ones'), rather in the way that children, and often parents too, have tended to view progress through an old-fashioned reading scheme. And further, perhaps the experience of choosing ought to include the possibility of making mistakes, provided that children do not find themselves abandoned without any frame of reference to work within. An appropriate compromise for picture books, used by some teachers, might be a system by which the books are informally classified into a few simple categories: hard, in between, and easy, for example. Or perhaps oral guidance by the teacher would suffice. Providing children with some help of this kind, without constraining choices by any very rigid system, should be sufficient in most classrooms. In addition, or alternatively, children could be taught the 'five-finger test' described by Baker.[3] The child chooses a page and begins to read it, and puts a finger on any word he or she cannot read. If he or she runs out of fingers on one hand before the end of the page, the book is probably too hard, and the child could decide to change it.

The final prerequisite, and one which is most important in this as in all aspects of the curriculum, is teachers' interest and enthusiasm − not only for picture books, but for the pleasure and value to be obtained from reading in general. With such enthusiasm so much can be achieved; without it all the preceding and following suggestions are really almost worthless.

Presenting Picture Books

Given teacher commitment, at least some attractive picture books and a physical environment which is as conducive to reading as conditions will allow, how can the teacher approach the task of introducing children to, and maintaining their interest in, a wide variety of good quality picture books?

Positive and Negative Practices

> Michael (aged 6): I like reading/but Mrs R don't she says you come and/read to me and then she starts shouting again.[4]

There are first a few practices seen in classrooms which seem fairly certain to have the opposite effects from those that are desirable. Sometimes, for example, from the best of motives teachers try to guide children away from books that seem inappropriate for one reason or another ('You're too old for that one, Stephen', 'You're not still reading those easy books, are you, David?', 'Really, Mary, it's time to try something different now'). We should perhaps be very cautious about making such comments. One of the characteristics of skilful and fluent readers of all ages is that they read at a variety of levels: as adults we sometimes like to read material that is as intellectually challenging and stimulating as we can cope with, but many of us also need much simpler reading for leisure and enjoyment. Very few adults want to read only and always books which are conceptually and structurally difficult; most of us like to relax with a Mills & Boon romance, or a thriller, or a magazine, or something similar. So we cannot reasonably expect children always to read at the limits of their ability. They too need the easy books and the pleasure of finishing a story quickly and comfortably.

An illustration from my own experience may reinforce the point. For the last thirty years I have kept a record of my own reading, and looking through it I find that the books I read now as an increasingly aged adult are in some respects rather different from those that I read as a child or as an adolescent. But the proportion of my reading then that could reasonably be described as serious and challenging is about the same as the proportion of material I read now which I find conceptually difficult. As a nine year old, much of my reading was of the dreaded Enid Blyton. A year or two later I read vast quantities of escapist fantasy by authors like Leslie Charteris and Dennis Wheatley. My current reading is largely of writers similarly lacking in high literary quality: Tom Sharpe, David Lodge, Len Deighton and similar material. So we should not rush children ahead too fast; better to wait, to let the children enjoy the security and the certainty of the familiar. They will in their own time reach out beyond their present reading boundaries (I don't read much Enid Blyton any more!).

Teachers should perhaps be cautious too about using picture books for other supposedly educational purposes. Books are sometimes ransacked for passages for comprehension or cloze exercises, or used as a means of giving spurious life to otherwise inanimate spelling and dictionary tests. Sometimes passages are copied out for handwriting practice, or incorporated wholesale and indiscriminately into topic or project work. Equally, teachers are sometimes tempted to impose a book on a child because other perhaps similar children have enjoyed it; yet children are individuals, with individual tastes and preferences. None of these practices is likely to increase children's desire to choose books eagerly and read them enthusiastically. Indeed, it is more likely that these are effective ways to turn children off reading!

To turn to the more positive, teachers can present stories and books to children in a variety of ways. The first and most obvious means is to read the story aloud as expressively and entertainingly as possible, to a class or to a smaller group. Listening to a story, whether or not the text is also available to the child, and talking about it afterwards, is an experience which all children should have as frequently as possible. There is no substitute for such a form of reading; it is the most important way in which children can grasp the shape and structure of stories, can as it were take hold of a book and make it their own, to be mentally reworked, adapted, thought through and finally absorbed as a complete experience.[5] Moira McKenzie has usefully summarized a number of ways in which such listening to and talking about stories is valuable. Among other benefits, she suggests, children can learn to

> Create images of scenes, actions and characters; identify key elements; experience feelings of joy, wonder, empathy, fear, hate, etc.; identify with particular people, places or events; relate stories to their personal lives and to other stories; project beyond the stories imaginatively – 'what if ...'; relate personal experiences to concepts and ideas; formulate personal viewpoints; learn how language is used in different kinds of discourse.[6]

Story telling has much the same value, but an ambience all its own; the text often takes on different and wider meanings when dramatically interpreted by a skilled storyteller. There is some recent evidence[7] that story telling is not much practised in classrooms, possibly because teachers find it difficult. If so, it is a great pity since it brings out very clearly the structure and coherence (and the magic) of a story. Teachers who are willing to learn the skills involved could profitably consult the recent book on the subject by Eileen Colwell and the very useful collection of short articles edited by Liz Weir.[8]

For both story reading and telling it is important that the physical conditions are as appropriate as possible. The children should be seated comfortably, and in a position where they can see the illustrations clearly. Many teachers ask children to sit on the floor around the teacher's chair, which is fine for a short period of time. It is usually best not to interrupt the narrative with comments and questions, but save them until the end. Let the story do its work first! And finally, it is important to give children time really to look at the pictures, and not hurry on to the next page too quickly; indeed, when teachers let the children dictate the pace of the reading, they are often surprised at how slowly they want to go!

Choosing and Using Books

Providing time for children to read is obviously crucial. As Jill Bennett, for many years a practising infant teacher, has said: 'Perhaps the most important factor in learning to read – apart from the books themselves – is TIME.'[9] Yet probably the most frustrating problem teachers face is the sheer lack of time to do all the things they would wish. Even though good classroom organization and management are helpful, unfortunately there is no complete solution. As Bennett goes on to say, in the end 'It is really a matter of priorities: time is needed, so I make time – although never enough.'[10] Clearly, the more it is possible for children to use and read books independently, the easier it is for the teacher to manage. While picture books are generally easier for children to read on their own, this is still likely to be a counsel of perfection with the youngest children. But as children get older they should be able to cope without so much direct or frequent guidance from the teacher. Baker makes a number of suggestions which she says could be duplicated in the form of a list and given to children to help them. For example: 'Choose a book that you already know. Books are often easier to read when you know the story first' and 'If you're reading a book and you find it gets boring, or too difficult, either finish it quickly and choose another, or change it at once.'[11]

Obviously, children can also read to the teacher from picture books, either instead of or as well as reading material from a more structured reading scheme. The practice of hearing individual children read to the teacher is very common, especially in infant classrooms, but this is not the place for a substantial analysis. Suffice it to say that there is evidence that longer but less frequent teacher–pupil reading conferences are of greater value than a daily reading which is often hurried and unsatisfactory because so many children must be 'heard' in a short time.[12] Such 'longer but less frequent' sessions suit picture books admirably, since it becomes feasible for teacher and child to read most or even all of a book together in the time available, rather than just a page or two brutally torn out of context.

Further, as I have stressed several times, one of the useful qualities of picture books for such work is that they naturally invite and encourage teacher and child (or child and child) to discuss as well as decode, to bring to bear not only their

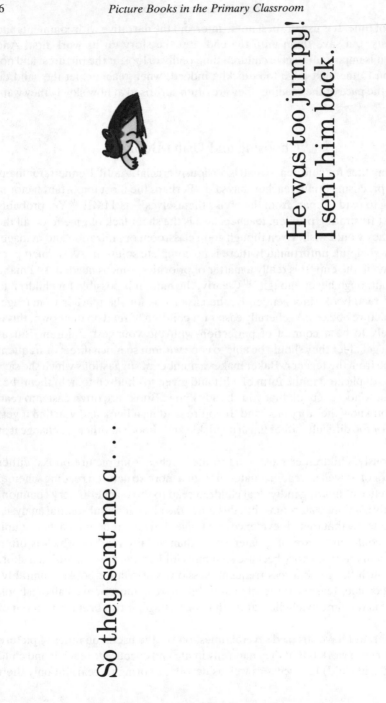

He was too jumpy!
I sent him back.

So they sent me a . . . .

Reprinted with permission from *Dear Zoo*, Rod Campbell, 1989, Campbell Books, London. First published 1982 by Abelard–Schuman Ltd.

linguistic but also their social and cultural knowledge. Colin Mills has recently provided a particularly interesting discussion of reading as such an essentially social process in the context of children's reading of David McKee's *Not Now, Bernard*, and the Ahlbergs' *Cops and Robbers*.[13] A similar example is provided by the following extract from a quite lengthy reading conference in which Ciara (aged five) reads the whole of Rod Campbell's *Dear Zoo* with her teacher. Ciara's attempts to read the text are in italics.

C: *So they sent me a . . . frog. He was too jumpy I sent him back.*
T: Yes would you like a frog for a pet?
C: No I had a frog in a field once.
T: Had you? Do they not make very good pets?
C: No they're all gone they were all . . . I had a tadpole for a while and you see they hadn't . . . the water was going to dry up 'cause it was summer and we put them in this wee bath that we kept water in it for them and then they all made frogs and then they all got out and they're away now.
T: Mm. So they jumped away did they? They were too jumpy!
C: *So they . . . so they thought very hard and sent me a . . . puppy! From your —*
T: All.
C: *All your friends at the zoo.*
T: Very good.
C: *He was just right. I kept him.*
T: Good. That word means just right. You had a very good guess at that word. But what . . . do you know what that word is really?
C: No.
T: He was per—
C: *Perfect.*
T: Perfect yes that means just right doesn't it?

Here we can see very clearly how a good picture book, with sufficient interest in the story and plenty of visual cues, provides excellent reading practice for the child. But also the reading provides an agenda for discussion, whereby Ciara can use her previous experience of frogs to help her make more sense of the topic; and thus the reading becomes a collaborative construction of meaning and not merely routine decoding practice.

Shared Reading

Another idea, perhaps somewhat less well known than 'hearing readers', is that of shared or paired reading. The thinking behind this technique is really very simple: if two children can share a copy of a picture book, the more skilled reader can read the story to his or her partner; or if both children can manage to read the story, they can take it in turns. This technique can be extended to groups of perhaps three or four children, and such groups can function very effectively for short to medium lengths of time. Some very useful resources for such work in the form of 'giant sized' versions of picture books have recently been published; these are ideal for a small group of children to look at together.[14]

The experience of shared reading is valuable both for the reader, who is practising his or her skill, and the read to, who is listening to a good story and following both words and pictures. (One of the partners in the shared reading could well be a parent.) In addition, this approach has the advantage of relieving some of the pressure on the teacher to listen to individual children reading very frequently. If children are reading to each other or to another adult regularly, the teacher may not need to feel obliged to 'hear readers' quite so often, thus releasing valuable teacher time for other activities.

A development and variation on this idea has recently become known by a number of different acronyms, such as USSR, SQUIRT, DEAR or even ERIC, all of which refer to the same basic idea: uninterrupted sustained silent reading, or everyone reading in class. This is to say that at regular intervals, and daily if possible, everyone in the class − and everyone must include the teacher − spends a few minutes reading or at least looking at a book of his or her choice (i.e. from school or home or anywhere else). Obviously the age and maturity of the children will determine both the length of time and the frequency, but schools adopting this system have regarded it as of great value.[15] Some schools have even extended the idea so that at a certain time everyone in the whole school, including headteacher, dinner ladies, caretaker and school secretary, is reading quietly!

The only point of all this is to ensure that each child is encouraged to spend a regular amount of class time reading; at the end of the day it does not matter a great deal what system the teacher uses, if any, as long as this purpose is achieved. Many teachers, of course do achieve it already, but others find that such quiet reading time is relentlessly squeezed by the demands of other areas of the curriculum. It may therefore be that the introduction (or even timetabling) of USSR would make it more difficult for the teacher to forget or mentally lose regular book reading under the pressure of everyday classroom life.

Audio-visual Presentation

There are many other ways of presenting stories, and particularly picture books, to children. There are excellent animated video versions of many popular picture books, including such favourites as *Rosie's Walk*, *The Snowman* and *Where the Wild Things Are*.[16] These are very useful, but rather expensive to buy. There are, however, other non-animated but equally effective videos containing versions of three or four picture books on each tape, making them rather more cost effective.[17] Even cheaper are the huge numbers of easily available story tapes,[18] in which a story or even a full-length novel is read by a professional actor. These tapes are of variable quality, but at their best are excellent for a small group of children to use alongside the book, either huddled round a tape recorder in some convenient stock cupboard, or listening with headphones at the back of the classroom. There are also a number of 'story-like' adventure computer programmes, the best of which complement picture books attractively and are delightful ways of stimulating imaginative and co-operative activities.[19]

Conclusion

In this chapter I have suggested several conditions and techniques for the effective use of picture books in the classroom. While contexts, resources and systems of classification are all significant, they often require long-term planning and organization. In the short term, it does seem important to provide children with a variety of literary experience. Even leaving aside practices which are in themselves not very constructive, almost any way of presenting stories and pictures to young children becomes tedious if repeated endlessly. But given a reasonable quantity of good picture books, a variety of ways of presenting them, and the all important teacher enthusiasm, children can benefit greatly.

Notes and References

1. Dean, J., *Room to Learn: Language Areas*, London, Evans, 1972.
2. Moss, E., *Picture Books for Young People 9—13* (2nd edn), Stroud, Thimble Press, 1988.
3. Baker, A., 'Developing reading with Juniors' in Moon, C. (ed.), *Practical Ways to Teach Reading*, London, Ward Lock, 1985, p. 17.
4. Quoted in Wade, B., 'Reading rickets and the uses of story', *English in Education*, Vol. 16, no. 3, 1982.
5. See, for example, Dombey, H., 'Partners in the telling', in Meek, M. and Mills, C. (eds.), *Language and Literacy in the Primary School*, Lewes, Falmer Press, 1988.
6. McKenzie, M., *Journeys into Literacy*, Huddersfield, Schofield & Sims, 1986, p. 18.
7. O'Kane, D., 'Once upon a time ...', *Education 3—13*, Vol. 17, no. 3, October 1989.
8. Colwell, E., *Storytelling*, London, Bodley Head, 1980; Weir, L., *Telling the Tale: A Storytelling Guide*, Youth Libraries Group, 1988.
9. Bennett, J., *Learning to Read with Picture Books* (3rd edn), Stroud, Thimble Press, 1985.
10. *Ibid.*, p. 8.
11. Baker, *op. cit.*, p. 17.
12. For detailed suggestions of appropriate strategies, see Arnold, H., *Listening to Children Reading*, Sevenoaks, Hodder & Stoughton, 1982.
13. Mills, C., 'Making sense of reading: Key Words or Grandma Swagg?', in Meek and Mills, *op. cit.*

14. 'Storytime Giants' are published by Oliver & Boyd, Longman House, Burnt Mill, Harlow, Essex CM20 2JE.

15. For further details, see Campbell, R., 'Is it time for USSR, SSR, SQUIRT, DEAR or ERIC?', *Education 3–13*, Vol. 16, no. 2, June 1988.

16. From Weston Woods, 14 Friday Street, Henley-on-Thames, Oxfordshire RG9 1AH.

17. From Reva Lee Studios, 96 Tolcarne Drive, Pinner, Middlesex HA5 2DP.

18. See Chapter 4, note 10.

19. Such as 'Dragon World' and 'Box of Treasures' from 4Mation Educational Resources, Linden Lea, Rock Park, Barnstaple, Devon.

Picture Books Mentioned in the Text

Ahlberg, J. and A., *Cops and Robbers*, Heinemann/Little Mammoth.
Briggs, R., *The Snowman*, Hamish Hamilton/Picture Puffin.
Campbell, R., *Dear Zoo*, Campbell Blackie/Picture Puffin.
Hutchins, P., *Rosie's Walk*, Bodley Head/Picture Puffin.
McKee, D., *Not Now, Bernard*, Andersen/Sparrow.
Sendak, M., *Where the Wild Things Are*, Bodley Head/Picture Puffin.

6
ACTIVITIES WITH PICTURE BOOKS

Frequently the experience of reading or being read to is enough. Books and readers interact in complex and rather mysterious ways, and thus further activities are often unnecessary. Certainly anything which intrudes between the child and his or her enjoyment of the book (for example, as mentioned earlier, using the text for handwriting practice or as a source for comprehension exercises, etc.) should be avoided. Equally frequently it is sufficient to give children the opportunity to talk about the experience that the book provides, whether one to one with the teacher, or with other children in a small group, or in a whole class setting.

But provided always that the picture book is not smothered in so much extraneous work that it gets lost, it may be that the experience of the book can be extended and deepened through follow-up activities used cautiously and with discrimination. Most of the kinds of follow-up work that are appropriate are very simple and straightforward, and are the kinds of activity that teachers might well engage in anyway as part of their everyday classroom work. Indeed, one of the attractions of picture books is that they naturally lend themselves to incorporation in all kinds of classroom activity.

It is obviously important to remember that only some of the following ideas may be relevant to any particular picture book, group of readers or classroom situation.

Activities for Beginning and Developing Readers

For beginning readers the more formally organized discussion strategies described later (p. 66) would probably be inappropriate, but certainly talking about the experience that picture books provide is of fundamental importance at any age or stage. Thus, for example, children could be asked to talk about specific aspects of a book they have read with a partner or in a small group. One of the picture books recently re-published in 'giant size' (such as the Ahlbergs' *ach Pear Plum*) would be ideal for this purpose, but the activity is not ..cult even with conventional picture books.

Almost all picture books provide lots of discussion points: for example, children could compare the morning routine in Jan Ormerod's *Sunshine* with their own; or think about the advantages and disadvantages of eating out of doors, following a reading of Sarah Garland's *Having a Picnic*; or describe their own pet's idiosyncrasies in the context of Eric Hill's Spot series. Alternatively, if children can have the experience of reading or hearing different versions of traditional stories like 'Little Red Riding Hood' or 'Noah and the Ark', one of which is in picture book format, it may be possible to discuss at a very simple level similarities and differences.

For the same reasons, *brief* class discussions could be held to review children's current reading at home and at school. Such discussions should enable children to say a little, if only a sentence or two, about what they are reading and their opinion of it. Perhaps following such discussions, each child could be encouraged to share a book he or she has enjoyed with a friend who has not looked at it before.

Children could make attractive covers for books. As well as drawing children's attention to some of the characteristics of books (title, author, publisher, etc.) that are often neglected, this provides some protection against the wear and tear of constantly being taken home and brought back again, or even getting kicked around the classroom floor!

The story of a picture book can be used as a stimulus for drama, movement, music or mime activities. Pat Hutchins' *Goodnight, Owl!* and the traditional story of 'The Three Billy Goats Gruff' are examples of books which can be very easily dramatized, using simple musical instruments to represent the characters. A picture book like David McKee's *Not Now, Bernard* can form the basis of effective mime. Slightly more complex stories like Jill Murphy's *On the Way Home* could also form the basis of an entertaining improvised performance.

Children could be asked to produce illustrations (with paint, crayon, charcoal or whatever is available) which thus create their own version of all or part of the story, or of their own story about the same characters. Very many picture books lend themselves to such activity. To mention only a few examples, children could follow a reading of Eric Carle's *The Mixed-Up Chameleon* by creating their own mixed-up animals; or after reading Oscar Wilde's *The Selfish Giant* children could paint pictures of the giant's garden at different times of the year. After looking at Sendak's *Where the Wild Things Are* children could invent their own monstrous creatures (and could also think up bizarre names for them!); or they could draw pictures with hiding places for objects or animals after reading the Zachariases' *But Where is the Green Parrot?* or the Ahlbergs' *Each Peach Pear Plum*.

Groups of children or the whole class could work together on a large wall frieze, mural or collage of scenes from a book like *The Snowman* or from parts of Briggs' *Father Christmas*. These are often particularly effective, as are zig-zag books telling a story (e.g. based on one of Nicoll and Pienkowski's Meg and Mog books).

Simple puppets based on the characters in a story are easy to make and are a very attractive means of developing children's manipulative skills; they can also be used dramatically as a way of encouraging appropriate oral expression (e.g. in the context of Rod Campbell's *Dear Zoo*, or the Berenstains' *Bears in the Night*). Shy and inarticulate children often find it easier to talk 'through' their puppet than speaking as themselves.

Writing a traditional book review is too difficult for most young children, and of doubtful value unless the written comments are only of a sentence or two. For the very youngest children, just a record of the title of the book, or a drawing of a favourite scene, accompanied by a drawing of a sad or smiling face to express a verdict may be sufficient. At this stage it is surely more appropriate for the children to express their ideas and opinions orally.

Tape recorders can be used profitably for individual children to record their reading of a favourite story. With the teacher's help, children could begin to think how such reading could be made expressive and interesting for the listener. Alternatively, and again with some guidance from the teacher, children could also perhaps tape record their opinions or discussion, and such tapes could be used by others as a source of reference when deciding on a new book to read.

Children could make their own simplified versions of lift-the-flap stories, such as the Spot series, with a few easily available resources (card, scissors, glue, etc.)

A whole class or large group of children could make their own alphabet book illustrating one or two letters each, possibly using one of the many published versions (e.g. John Burningham's *Alphabet Book*) as stimulus. Alternatively, each child could contribute to a counting book, perhaps using *Anno's Counting Book* as a starting point (see also Appendix 2, pp. 133–40 for other simple alphabet and number books).

Another interesting whole-class activity is for children collectively and orally to make up their own story about picture book characters or situations, which the teacher transcribes on to the blackboard or into a large folder (or on to a computer word processor system). For example, with help from the teacher children could make up stories about 'Caterpillar's Walk', or 'Not Now, Susan', or 'Meg and Mog at Park Lane School', or whatever. This is a particularly valuable activity because children can learn something of the nature and problems of writing stories, and in particular the need for drafting and redrafting, without getting totally bogged down in the physical struggle with pencils and rubbers, or by the need to rely solely on their own resources for plot or dialogue since the original story provides a useful framework. Children often take great delight in such collective stories, and they can provide a real sense of authorship.

Children are often fascinated by names, both their own and other people's. Characters in picture books often have interesting names, and children could therefore be asked to think of suitable names for pirates (e.g. in the context of Pat Hutchins' *One Eyed Jake*) or dinosaurs (Helen Piers' *Long Neck and Thunderfoot*) or unusual creatures (Hiawyn Oram's *Ned and the Joybaloo*), or, even easier, bears or pigs or cats.

Picture books on a similar theme could contribute towards a class exploration of a topic (see Appendix 2, pp. 133—40 for some suggestions). A whole-school project on Roald Dahl's *The Enormous Crocodile* has recently been described,[1] and many other themes (such as colour, mice and bears) have been discussed as possibilities for simple topics centred on picture books.[2] Picture books can make a valid contribution to such investigations. For example, books like Helen Oxenbury's *Gran and Grandpa*, Peter Smith's *Jenny's Baby Brother* and Shirley Hughes' Alfie series could be used in the study of families and relationships. Another possibility would be to use such books as David McKee's *Two Monsters* and Helen Piers' *Long Neck and Thunderfoot* as a basis for children to consider questions of conflict and co-operation. Similarly, there are many picture books which can contribute towards children's mathematical development as well as being enjoyable in their own right: for example, a book like *The Bad Tempered Ladybird* could lead to useful work on time and timetables, and *Anno's Counting Book* provides an innovative approach to learning simple numbers.

Some picture books provide a multiplicity of starting points for thematic work. For example, the Ahlbergs' *The Baby's Catalogue* could lead to discussion and activities on the theme of brothers and sisters and family relationships, or to the topic of catalogues and other reference systems like dictionaries and timetables, or to work on human development and growth.

A very useful activity has been suggested by the authors of guidance for the implementation of the National Curriculum provisions for English, Key Stage 1. The idea is worth quoting at length:

> Children can be encouraged to think of watching television or films, or looking at pictures, as a kind of 'reading'. By looking closely at visual images and discussing exactly what they can see (use the stop-frame device on the video) children can begin to see how most still and moving images are organised on purpose, and how visual conventions and symbols are used.[3]

The authors go on to provide details of interesting and useful work involving children taking photographs of each other and then discussing and using the resulting prints;[4] certainly much valuable talking and listening can emerge from such activities.

An activity which many young children much enjoy is to follow the 'career' of a picture book character through different stories. Such books are also very useful for the beginning reader, since he or she does not have to come to terms with a new set of conventions and styles each time: the framework of the story is already in place. Authors and publishers, of course, appreciate this, and produce series of books, many of which are reviewed or referred to in Chapters 8–11. Some of the books which are particularly suitable for reading serially in this way are those about Spot (Hill), Mr Bear (Kuratomi), King Rollo (McKee), Meg and Mog (Nicoll and Pienkowski), Alfie (Hughes), Mog (Kerr), Frog and Toad (Lobel) and the Teddybears (Gretz). It may be easier for children to invent their own oral, written or artistic versions of the character's adventures when they have available such a range of exemplars.

Many picture books (such as lift-the-flap books) naturally require children to predict and anticipate. With others, however, it may be useful sometimes to ask the children to try to tell all or part of the story (or just the ending) without reading the text or having it read to them first. 'What do you think is going to happen next?' is always a useful question.

There are a number of activities focused on picture books which children can undertake in odd moments, wet playtimes and similar occasions. For example, if the teacher has the time and energy, he or she can create simple word games, such as crosswords using characters' names (Mog, Spot, Rosie, etc.) or wordsearch puzzles in which children are asked to find words from a particular text (e.g. the numbers from Pomerantz's *One Duck, Another Duck*).

Activities for Extending and Independent Readers

Obviously many of the activities outlined above can be valuable for older children too, but slightly more sophisticated ideas for work arising out of picture books can also be devised; in turn, many of these can be adapted for use with younger children.

Activities which invite children to predict and anticipate are very useful. For example, a picture book (such as Chris Van Allsburg's *The Wreck of the Zephyr*) could be presented to children without the text, and they could be asked to write all or part of the story line to accompany the pictures. Alternatively, the story could be read without the children seeing the pictures, and they could be asked to predict the contents of the illustrations.

All or some of the pictures from a wordless book (e.g. *Sunshine* by Jan Ormerod) could be presented to a group of children in a random order; their task is to reassemble the story, and to provide reasons for their choices. This again is a useful activity for prediction.[5]

For children to tell the story of a wordless picture book is a particularly useful activity because the child is invited by such a task to be creative, yet is provided with a helpful framework. Children's attempts may also provide the teacher with worthwhile information about their ability to handle narrative.[6]

Children could be asked to consider what is lost if the pictures are taken away and only the text remains. Are the illustrations essential to the story? What do they add to it? Is it possible to replace the pictures with more text, and if this is done, how is the book different?

Teachers or preferably the children themselves could construct agendas of questions about a book for discussion in pairs or groups. Obviously, appropriate questions vary according to the picture book chosen, and according to the age and attainments of the children. In general, however, they could focus on such themes as the nature and behaviour of the characters, the context of the story, the sequence of events, the point of the story, and the style of writing and illustrations. Also, different types of question could be included. For example, in relation to *Come Away from the Water, Shirley*:

- Closed questions, those to which there is really only one right answer: e.g. who was Shirley's companion in her adventures?
- Open questions, to which there are a limited range of reasonable answers: e.g. why did Shirley's Mum keep nagging her?
- Enabling questions, where there is no right answer, but answers are, within reason, a matter of opinion: e.g. who do you think enjoyed their day at the beach most, and why?

Thus, for example, in relation to Anthony Browne's *Gorilla*, a wonderful picture book for older primary school children, groups of children could be asked to consider a few questions such as:

- Why was Hannah's Dad so busy?
- Why did Hannah throw the toy gorilla into a corner?
- What did Hannah think when she saw the huge gorilla?
- Can you work out what 'primates' means?
- Why did Hannah think the orang-utan and chimpanzee were sad?
- What was the film about that Hannah and the gorilla went to see?
- Which are the most interesting pictures in the book, and why?
- What are the advantages and disadvantages of keeping animals in zoos?
- Should animals be kept as pets?

It is not difficult to construct agendas, and increasingly as children become more skilled at discussion they also become better at thinking of appropriate questions to ask themselves.

Discussions can then be held based on these agendas. At first these should only consider one or two questions, for just a few minutes (five at most), and in groups of two or three children. The number and complexity of questions, the length of time and the group size can be increased as pupils become more skilled at the activity. Groups could report back selectively to the whole class if this is appropriate and/or could tape their deliberations.

Such activities are very valuable because discussion is one of the fundamental ways in which we all learn. However, careful organization is necessary, especially with children who have not engaged in much group work before. Some teachers have tried discussions in their classrooms and, finding that there are difficulties, have retreated back into written 'comprehension' questions and similar work. But it is worth persisting, even if classroom management poses problems initially. Children do need practice in order to become skilled at the techniques and conventions required, just as they need practice at any other sophisticated activity. But if any teachers are unconvinced of the value of discussion, it should be noted that the National Curriculum for English *requires* that 'speaking and listening' attainment targets be met!

While on the subject of the National Curriculum, the authors make useful suggestions regarding the use of what is called 'media education' in the context of speaking and listening. For example, they suggest that children might compare black and white with coloured pictures and discuss the differences that the choice of medium makes; or take photographs and make tapes to express ideas and feelings and develop critical reflection.[7]

Although the traditional book review is generally an activity of doubtful value, children could be asked occasionally to write an account which is both brief and structured. If the activity is given a specific purpose (i.e. to provide information about the book to someone who has not read it) and then actually used as such, it becomes more meaningful. An example of a simple format, which can obviously be varied to suit children of greater or lesser writing ability, follows on p. 68.

Publicity for the book can be devised: for example, a poster for the 'film of the book' (such as Keeping's *The Highwayman*, or Lindgren's *The Ghost of Skinny Jack*) could be made as realistically as possible, i.e. incorporating film stars' names, critics' views, performance times and so on: 'Now Showing', 'Nominated for Eight Oscars', 'Must Close This Week', etc.

Many children enjoy making a map or plan of the area of the book's action: an interesting activity for a book like *Come Away from the Water, Shirley*, or Rodney Peppe's *The Kettleship Pirates*. In the case of a book like Waddell and Dupasquier's *Going West*, children could even follow the action of the book across a map of the USA.

The design of book jackets can be a bit more complex than those attempted with younger children, to include the blurb on the back, publisher's name, title and author on spine, ISBN number, etc. Other details, such as copyright notice,

---

BOOK REVIEW

Title of book:_____ Author's name:_____

Illustrator's name:_____ Publisher:_____

The story was about _____

_____

_____

_____

_____

This is a picture of the best part of the story:

I thought the book was
brilliant
good
all right
not very good
terrible

because_____

_____

_____

Signed:_____   _____

---

publisher's details, dedication and contents page, could also usefully be examined in their own right. As Baker has argued, 'As children come to appreciate how books work, their power to use them grows.'[8]

Several picture books of similar theme could be used as the centre of a brief and focused comparison of different authors' treatment of character, setting or theme. The topics chosen could vary from the fairly concrete (like school, treasure or weather) to the more abstract (such as loneliness, family relationships or conservation). For example, what are the similarities and differences between both the journeys described and the family relationships implied in *Jyoti's Journey* (Ganly), *Are We Nearly There?* (Baum) and *Dear Daddy ...* (Dupasquier)? Or what are the implications for conservation of books like *Professor Noah's Spaceship* (Wildsmith) and *Dinosaurs and All That Rubbish* (Foreman)?

Similarly, a selection of picture books on a theme such as the sea, or time, or colours could contribute a distinctive dimension to mathematical or simple scientific activities or environmental studies. For example, *The Mixed-Up Chameleon* (Carle) and *How the Birds Changed Their Feathers* (Troughton) could be very useful for work on the topic of colour. See also Appendix 2, pp. 133–40, where some picture books are indexed by theme.

Children could also discuss the different ways in which a theme is treated in a picture story book and in non-fiction. What are the differences and similarities between, say, Margaret Andrew and Tracey Lewis's amusing picture book about a dancing penguin, called *Mac the Macaroni*, and Oxford Scientific Films' real life portrayal in *The Penguin in the Snow* (Methuen)? Or any of the myriad factual books about dinosaurs could be compared with a picture book like Helen Piers' *Long Neck and Thunderfoot*. Similarly, children could examine the contrast between stories by an author and his or her own real life: see, for example, Roald Dahl's autobiographical *Boy* and *Going Solo* (Puffin).

Picture books based more or less closely on famous stories, such as 'Noah's Ark' (e.g. *Norah's Ark* by Cartwright), 'Hiawatha' (*Hiawatha's Childhood* by Longfellow), 'Treasure Island' (*The Kettleship Pirates* by Peppe), 'Jack and the Beanstalk' (*Jim and the Beanstalk* by Briggs) or 'Gulliver's Travels' (*The Return of the Antelope* by Hoffman) could be usefully compared with the originals. Or alternatively, traditional versions of stories like 'Goldilocks' or 'Little Red Riding Hood' could be compared with newer versions, like those in Roald Dahl's *Revolting Rhymes*. All such efforts of comparison and contrast could provide interesting questions for a discussion agenda.

A number of picture books are particularly useful for older children who find reading difficult; many of them are in cartoon style (such as the Stanley Bagshaw, Tintin and Asterix books; see also Appendix 3, p. 141, for further suggestions). One advantage of such strip cartoon books is that they do not seem babyish; after all, many children who can read well are reading comics of similar appearance. Another advantage is that, even more than in picture books generally, the structure and framework of the strip provides great help to the struggling reader, and carries him or her along, even if the text is quite difficult. And further support is often provided by the fact that characters and situations do not have to be learnt afresh for each book, and thus activities which emphasize continuity and the 'career' of characters can be attempted.

Children could be encouraged to talk about a favourite picture book to a group or to the class as a whole. Initially, such talks may last only thirty seconds or so, and indicate just the author, title, illustrator, main character(s), one theme of the story, and a personal opinion of the book as a whole. With practice, children should be able to extend the duration and complexity of their talks. Obviously, it is not only the speaker who has skills to learn in this type of work; the audience too has to understand how to respond appropriately and constructively to each presentation.

It is worth asking children to keep a record of all their reading: a simple list of authors and titles, plus a 'star rating' (from one star to a maximum of five, perhaps). Or children could make their own individual list of 'My Top Ten Books', or a collective class list could be voted for from time to time and displayed in the classroom. At least one school uses a system known as 'Can You Judge' to indicate preferences:

 0 Catastrophic
 1 Awful
 2 No, not really
 3 You have to be desperate
 4 Only just
 5 U may find it satisfactory
 6 Just about getting there
 7 U should enjoy it
 8 Definitely a good read
 9 Great!
10 Explosively and amazingly brilliant!

All such activities of recording and assessing are interesting for children, and it is useful for the teacher to have a record of the way individuals' reading choices are (or are not!) developing over time. It is even possible to make use of children's ratings to construct histograms or pictograms to represent class opinions in a graphic form.

A 'radio programme' could be made on tape about a book, incorporating the reading of an extract, an interview with a child who has read the book, a discussion between children with differing opinions, bibliographical information, etc. Alternatively, children could be asked to think about which five books they would take with them as a castaway on a desert island, and could also provide reasons for their choices. A class version of the famous radio programme ('Desert Island Books') might then be made on tape.

Alternatively, a newspaper-style format could be adopted, as in the review pages of real journals or magazines. The children could construct a front page with headlines, reports, 'photographs', advertisements, etc.

Children who can read fairly fluently could make tape recordings of stories, to be listened to by those who are younger and/or less skilful; or, of course, children could occasionally be asked to read in person to a group in another class.

Following a reading of Judith Crabtree's *The Sparrow's Story at the King's Command*, in which the initial letters of each page are decorated in the style of medieval manuscripts, children could write and decorate similarly their own alphabet book or a copy of a favourite poem or passage.

Children's own illustrated stories can be 'published'. With the increased availability in schools in recent years of microcomputers with word processing or even desktop publishing facilities, such ventures are quite easily managed, although hand- or type-written versions which are then photocopied are, of course, perfectly adequate. Children's published stories can be a very useful reading resource for the writer (who has at least one book that he or she can read confidently) and for other children, not only in the same class.

Letters must be for real, to communicate, otherwise they are arid and meaningless. Learning how to lay out letters is important, but it is a means to an end, not an end in itself. Letters could be written describing or commenting on a favourite book and sent to a friend in another class or school, perhaps as part of a wider exchange; the Ahlbergs' *The Jolly Postman* could be a particularly useful resource for all such work. Or children could write to the author (via the publisher) expressing appreciation, asking questions, etc. Most writers of children's books will respond enthusiastically, although in fairness they should not be deluged with hundreds of letters! This is a particularly useful exercise, and one that children find very exciting because it helps them to realize that books do not just appear out of thin air, but are written and illustrated by real, and ordinary, people just like the ones they know.

A particularly valuable activity is to look at the ways in which illustrators consciously use pictures to convey meanings which extend and modify what is said in the text. *Rosie's Walk* is a classic example, of course, but many picture books use the technique to a greater or lesser extent. For example, in David McKee's *Not Now, Bernard* the whole point of the story is that pictures and words provide contradictory messages. And in a rather more complex way much of the humour of Graham Oakley's *Church Mouse* series derives from the comparison, and often contrast, between what is said in the deadpan text and what is shown in the witty pictures.

Children might collect examples of a favourite illustrator's work (e.g. Maurice Sendak, Michael Foreman, Quentin Blake or Charles Keeping, who illustrate their own as well as other writers' books). More ambitiously, children could be asked to compare and contrast pictures by different illustrators: it is clear, for example, that Jan Pienkowski's pictures are quite unlike those of the Ahlbergs or John Burningham; the work of Babette Cole is very different from that of

Errol Le Cain. But how can the differences be described; in terms of line, or colour, or theme, or medium? How, for example, do line drawings differ from paintings, and differ again from collage? How are all such illustrations different from photographs? Does it make sense to consider to what extent different illustrators' pictures are realistic? What effect has the deliberate use of black and white illustrations? By thinking about such questions it may be possible to move beyond saying merely, 'I like that picture but not that one', towards a thoughtful (but brief) discussion of the strengths and limitations of styles, techniques or media. Again, such questions could form an agenda for discussion, and through such activities children can learn something about the nature of critical artistic judgement, and how and why individual opinions and preferences can vary.

An activity that is very popular with children is to collect examples of humour from different picture books. It may be possible in addition to begin to categorize and classify different types of humour: for example, some books are funny mainly because of aspects of their plot, or use of language, or characterization (e.g. Jeanne Willis's *The Tale of Fearsome Fritz*, or Roy Gerrard's *Sir Cedric*), others derive much of their humour from the absurdity or wit of the illustrations (such as Babette Cole's *Nungu and the Crocodile* or the work of Quentin Blake); yet others are funny because of the comic interaction between what is said in the text and what is shown in the illustrations (as in much of Colin and Jacqui Hawkins' work, and in Oakley's Church Mouse series referred to above).

There are, as described earlier,[9] animated and non-animated video versions of some well-known picture books. If children could experience both book and video, they could then be asked to discuss the differences and similarities, and/ or to construct a list of the advantages and disadvantages of each medium for the story.

A rather ambitious project, but one which can be undertaken with a class of any age or attainment, or even as a whole school activity, is to hold a book fair. Some schools organize such an event to coincide with National Book Week, and use a visit by an author of children's books as the centrepiece of, or the finale to, the event.[10]

Some teachers organize competitions in which children are asked to answer questions relating to books through investigations in the school and/or public library, perhaps over the period of a school holiday; such activities are fun, provided that they are not too difficult for the children, or done too often! Obviously, questions should be varied to suit the experience and capabilities of the children, but the following are examples:

* Name three picture books written and illustrated by John Burningham.
* Who has written a series of books featuring Stanley Bagshaw?
* Who or what is . . . ?

- Name five picture book titles by different authors that include the word 'bear'.
- Which book or books feature characters named: Tiddalik; Fungus; Songololo; Nungu; Officer Pugh; Len the Laugher; Celestine?
- What have the following in common: *Mouse Trouble*; *The Rain Door*; *The Enormous Crocodile*?
- How many picture book versions of the story of Noah can you name?

As with younger children, there are a number of simple puzzle-type activities which can be used during odd moments of the school day, or during wet playtimes. More complex crossword puzzles and wordsearch patterns can be created, using names of characters from a variety of familiar picture books, or just words from a particular text. Alternatively, children could be asked to find as many words as possible using the letters in a character's name (Gumdrop, Asterix). Children themselves might be able to create simple board games with characters and situations from picture books, or make jigsaw puzzles by pasting a copy of a favourite illustration on to heavy card and then carefully cutting it up.

Another possible puzzle activity would be to ask children to find a character, or an animal, or a title from picture books to fit each letter of the alphabet. For example, titles might include A for *Asterix the Gaul*, B for *Burglar Bill*, C for *Clotilda's Magic*, etc; or animal characters might include A for antelope (in *The Return of the Antelope*), B for bear (in *How Do I Put It On?*), C for cat (in *Mog and the Baby*), and so on.

Finally, two wonderful books for wet playtimes: Mike Wilks' *The Ultimate Alphabet Book* consists of hundreds and hundreds of objects to spot within its 26 pictures (one for each letter of the alphabet); and Malcolm Bird's *The Witch's Handbook* is full of very funny ideas and illustrations. It is well worth investing in a classroom copy of each of these as they will entertain children of any age (and their teachers!) for hours.

Conclusion

The only valid reason for any or all activities in the classroom which follow the reading of picture books is to extend and develop enjoyment and understanding; other motives or purposes are likely to do more harm than good. Indeed, there is no need for teachers to feel almost guilty if children read, or have read to them, a picture book which they obviously enjoy, but do no follow-up activities at all. In particular, written work is not always necessary. The view that children only really learn anything if they write endlessly about it is contrary to common sense, let alone educational research! The activities suggested above should therefore be used sparingly, when and if appropriate, and with professional sensitivity. So used they can be of great value.

Notes and References

1. In *Child Education*, Vol. 66, no. 4, April 1989.
2. Thomas, R. and Perry, A., *Into Books: 101 Literature Activities for the Classroom*, Melbourne, Oxford University Press, 1984.
3. National Curriculum Council, *English Key Stage 1: Non-Statutory Guidance*, York, National Curriculum Council, 1989, p. C12, section 8.11.
4. *Ibid.*, p. C21.
5. Both these first two ideas come from Benton, M. and Fox, G., *Teaching Literature Nine to Fourteen*, Oxford University Press, 1985.
6. An interesting example in relations to Raymond Briggs' *The Snowman* is provided in Fry, D., *Children Talk About Books: Seeing Themselves as Readers*, Milton Keynes, Open University Press, 1985, pp. 17–21, 110–11.
7. National Curriculum Council, *op. cit.*, p. C7, section 4.9.
8. Baker, A., 'Developing reading with Juniors', in Moon, C. (ed.), *Practical Ways to Teach Reading*, London, Ward Lock, 1985, p. 17.
9. See chapter 5, notes 16 and 17.
10. For an example, see Short, H., *Bright Ideas: Using Books in the Classroom*, Leamington Spa, Scholastic Publications, 1989, p. 111.

Picture Books Mentioned in the Text

Ahlberg, J. and A., *Each Peach Pear Plum*, Viking Kestrel/Picture Lion.
Ahlberg, J. and A., *The Baby's Catalogue*, Viking Kestrel/Picture Puffin.
Ahlberg, J. and A., *Burglar Bill*, Heinemann/Little Mammoth.
Ahlberg, J. and A., *The Jolly Postman*, Heinemann.
Andrew, M., *Mac the Macaroni*, Macdonald.
Anno, M., *Anno's Counting Book*, Picturemac.
Baum, L., *Are We Nearly There?*, Bodley Head/Magnet.
Berenstain, S. and J., *Bears in the Night*, Collins.
Bird, M., *The Witch's Handbook*, Beaver.
Briggs, R., *The Snowman*, Hamish Hamilton/Picture Puffin.
Briggs, R., *Father Christmas*, Hamish Hamilton/Picture Puffin.
Briggs, R., *Jim and the Beanstalk*, Picture Puffin.
Browne, A., *Gorilla*, Julia MacRae/Little Mammoth.
Burningham, J., *Alphabet Book*, Walker.
Burningham, J., *Come Away from the Water, Shirley*, Cape/Picture Lion.
Campbell, R., *Dear Zoo*, Campbell Blackie/Picture Puffin.
Carle, E., *The Bad Tempered Ladybird*, Hamish Hamilton/Picture Puffin.
Carle, E., *The Mixed-Up Chameleon*, Hamish Hamilton/Picture Puffin.
Cartwright, A., *Norah's Ark*, Hutchinson/Picture Puffin.
Cole, B., *Nungu and the Crocodile* (out of print).
Crabtree, J., *The Sparrow's Story at the King's Command*, Oxford University Press.
Dahl, R., *Revolting Rhymes*, Cape/Picture Puffin.
Dahl, R., *The Enormous Crocodile*, Cape/Picture Puffin.
Dupasquier, P., *Dear Daddy . . .*, Andersen/Picture Puffin.
Foreman, M., *Dinosaurs and All That Rubbish*, Picture Puffin.
Ganly, H., *Jyoti's Journey*, Deutsch.
Garland, S., *Having a Picnic*, Bodley Head/Picture Puffin.

Gerrard, R., *Sir Cedric*, Gollancz.
Goscinny, R., Asterix series, Hodder & Stoughton.
Gretz, S., Teddybears series, A & C Black/Picture Lion.
Hergé, Tintin series, Methuen.
Hill, E., Spot series, Heinemann/Picture Puffin.
Hoban, R., *The Rain Door*, Gollancz/Picturemac.
Hoffman, M., *The Return of the Antelope*, Heinemann/Picture Puffin.
Hughes, S., Alfie series, Bodley Head/Picture Lion.
Hutchins, P., *Rosie's Walk*, Bodley Head/Picture Puffin.
Hutchins, P., *One Eyed Jake*, Bodley Head/Picture Puffin.
Hutchins, P., *Goodnight, Owl*, Bodley Head/Picture Puffin.
Keeping, C., *The Highwayman*, Oxford University Press.
Kent, J., *Clotilda's Magic* (out of print).
Kerr, J., Mog series, Collins/Picture Lion.
Kuratomi, C., Mr Bear series, Macdonald.
Lindgren, A., *The Ghost of Skinny Jack*, Methuen.
Lobel, A., Frog and Toad series, World's Work/Young Puffin.
Longfellow, H., *Hiawatha's Childhood*, Faber/Picture Puffin.
McKee, D., *Not Now, Bernard*, Andersen/Sparrow.
McKee, D., King Rollo series, Andersen.
McKee, D., *Two Monsters*, Andersen/Beaver.
Murphy, J., *On the Way Home*, Macmillan/Picturemac.
Nicoll, H. and Pienkowski, J., Meg and Mog series, Heineman/Picture Puffin.
Oakley, G., Church Mouse series, Macmillan/Picturemac.
Oram, H., *Ned and the Joybaloo*, Andersen/Beaver.
Ormerod, J., *Sunshine*, Picture Puffin.
Oxenbury, H., *Gran and Grandpa*, Walker.
Peppe, R., *The Kettleship Pirates*, Viking Kestrel/Picture Puffin.
Piers, H., *Long Neck and Thunderfoot*, Viking Kestrel/Picture Puffin.
Pomerantz, C., *One Duck, Another Duck*, Picture Puffin.
Sendak, M., *Where the Wild Things Are*, Bodley Head/Picture Puffin.
Smith, P., *Jenny's Baby Brother*, Picture Lion.
Troughton, J., *How the Birds Changed Their Feathers*, Blackie.
Van Allsburg, C., *The Wreck of the Zephyr*, Andersen/Picture Puffin.
Waddell, M., *Going West*, Andersen/Picture Puffin.
Watanabe, S., *How Do I Put It On?*, Bodley Head/Picture Puffin.
Wilde, O., *The Selfish Giant*, Kaye & Ward/Picture Puffin.
Wildsmith, B., *Professor Noah's Spaceship*, Oxford University Press.
Wilks, M., *The Ultimate Alphabet Book*, Pavilion.
Willis, J., *The Tale of Fearsome Fritz*, Andersen/Beaver.
Wilson, B., Stanley Bagshaw series, Hamish Hamilton/Picture Puffin.
Yeoman, J., *Mouse Trouble*, Picture Puffin.
Zacharias, T. and W., *But Where is the Green Parrot?*, Bodley Head/Picture Piper.

PART II
REVIEWS

7
(SOME OF) THE BEST PICTURE BOOKS

Sources of Information

Finding out about children's books is not difficult: indeed, there is a plethora of material available from a great many sources.

Local Sources

First of all there are sources within the school itself. Children and parents may, and colleagues almost certainly will, know books that the teacher has not come across before (and might even be willing to lend copies). Also within the school there are often catalogues from publishers which contain useful articles and other material as well as details of the particular company's literary offerings.[1] Various general educational journals and magazines often found in staffrooms (such as *Child Education*, *Junior Education* and *The Times Educational Supplement*) regularly carry reviews and articles about aspects of children's fiction.

The local public library is a wonderful place to discover new books and copies of old favourites. Quite apart from the possibility of borrowing copies of what may be prohibitively expensive books for use in the classroom, any books that are not immediately available can be ordered through the library system. Teachers can thus have a good look at a wide variety of titles and make sure which ones are really what is wanted before deciding to buy copies for school; or even better, they can take children to the library to choose the books they are really interested in. This is obviously much more satisfactory than relying on catalogue descriptions. Do not neglect too the expertise and knowledge that public librarians have at their fingertips; as I have happily discovered while writing this book, they can save the teacher hours of searching for elusive books on particular themes or for particular children. And, just as important, librarians are by the nature of their work enthusiasts for books and reading, and are almost always willing to share their enthusiasm with teachers. A local librarian who is particularly interested in children's books is an ally that the teacher should cultivate!

Teachers who wish to take a deeper interest in children's books will find no shortage of material. There are several useful (and free) general catalogues of children's books in print,[2] which are somewhat less forbidding than exhaustive works like the *British National Bibliography*, or *British Books in Print on Microfiche*, which can, however, be consulted in any major public library.

Journals and Magazines

A large number of local, national and even international journals and magazines are published devoted to children's books in all their variety. Local and regional magazines are often particularly interesting and useful: examples include the former ILEA's *Tried and Tested*,[3] *Children's Books in Ireland*[4] and the *Essex Review of Children's Literature*.[5] All such magazines are constantly looking for contributions by teachers, and would welcome contact. Of course, if no such journal exists locally, it would be well worth thinking about starting one; it is really not very difficult!

National magazines are both plentiful and very varied. *Books for Keeps*[6] is perhaps one of the best for teacher enthusiasts as it includes plenty of short reviews of new books for children of all ages, as well as interviews with authors and lots of other interesting features. It is also inexpensive, very attractively produced, and written in a lively and accessible style. A national and international journal of rather different character is *Children's Literature in Education*.[7] It generally publishes substantial articles and essays: studies of particular texts or authors, accounts of practice in schools, and analyses of the nature of literary response. Serious certainly, even academic in the best sense, but often fascinating reading.

Books

It sometimes seems as if there are as many books about children's literature as there are children's books to write about (and this is yet one more!). Interested teachers will no doubt explore the Bibliography on pp. 142–43, but at this point it may be worth drawing attention to just one or two examples of each of a few different types of book, focusing mainly on those books particularly relevant to the teacher of younger children.

An excellent general guidebook to the best children's books, for all ages and including non-fiction as well as fiction, is Taylor and Braithwaite's *The Good Book Guide to Children's Books*, which includes some six hundred chirpy and snappy reviews, well illustrated with colour and black and white pictures (full details of this and the following recommended books will be found in the Bibliography). Dorothy Butler's *Babies Need Books* has already been mentioned; the title indicates and summarizes the contents, and it is an excellent read. Also aimed primarily at parents are Margaret Meek's *Learning to Read*, full of a lifetime's experience of books and children, and Jim Trelease's *The Read-Aloud Handbook*. Both are very useful, although I would dispute Trelease's assertions about the supposedly unmitigated evils of television. Peggy Heeks' *Choosing and Using Books in the First School*, Thomas and Perry's *Into Books: 101 Literature Activities for the Classroom* and Branston and Provis's *Children and Parents Enjoying Reading* contain useful ideas and resources for teachers of young children, as does the Open University Team's in-service education pack called *Children, Language and Literature*. Volume 1 of this latter publication contains a wide variety of interesting articles, and volume 2 (*Finding Out about Children's Books*) consists of no fewer than fifty pages of bibliographical material and other information and help for teachers.

Busy teachers may not have much time to read historical, literary or educational studies of children's books, or volumes of research into aspects of children's reading, but for those who have, some recent examples are listed in the Bibliography. A good place to start investigating the empirical research literature is Southgate *et al.*'s *Extending Beginning Reading*, a fascinating and thoughtful piece of work. Recent and particularly rewarding studies of children's books are John Rowe Townsend's *Written for Children* (third edition), an entertaining and well-written account of the history of children's books including substantial sections on picture books; John Spink's interesting study, *Children as Readers*; and Michele Landsberg's *The World of Children's Books*, which attempts to analyse the whole vast range of children's fiction and recommend titles that are really excellent – not an easy task!

An Adventure of the Spirit

In an earlier chapter I quoted Liz Waterland's comment that books should be seen as an end in themselves, rather than as only a means by which children learn to read. She goes on:

> We are hoping to offer the world of literature to children; to show even the youngest, least mature beginner in books that within the covers of a loved book is an adventure of the spirit – something that can speak to that child alone and lead her or him into a wider world.[8]

In the reviews that follow, therefore, the attempt has been made to pick out and recommend some of the picture books that seem to offer such an 'adventure of the spirit' to the child reader, and which also offer the teacher some personal and professional stimulation.

Types of Picture Book

Certain categories of book have been excluded from consideration. Most books written with the intention of being straightforwardly informative, however appropriately illustrated they may be, clearly fall outside the scope of this work, with the exception that some simple alphabet books and counting books have been retained. For similar reasons, none of the beautifully illustrated collections of verse for children have been included[9] although room has been found for some stories told in verse and for a few books of nursery rhymes. This is not, of course, to deny the importance of either poetry or reading for information; both have significant parts to play in children's literary experience.

Even with these exclusions, however, the attempt to pick the 'best' picture books remains rather ambitious. There are still thousands of books to choose from and it is difficult to keep up with the new ones as they are published, let alone read the huge range and variety of existing material. Further, of course, the fact that no two readers' assessments of what is a good book are ever likely to coincide completely is in one sense part of the delight of reading at all, but it also causes problems for the reviewer! Thus for one reason or another both teachers and children may well find that some of their favourite titles are missing.

It is not easy to categorize different types of picture book. Perhaps the most obvious form of classification of children's literature, including picture books, is by topic (dinosaurs, bears, houses and homes, ghosts and witches, and so on). But as Warlow has pointed out,[10] this is often rather unsatisfactory, since it results in the lumping together of books which are very superficially related but much more fundamentally different. Warlow goes on to suggest a rather more complex scheme by which books are classified according to the extent to which they maintain, amend or ignore the 'normal laws of nature'.[11] Such a form of categorization is interesting, but its practical value to the classroom teacher is not entirely clear. In the case of books for very young children, for example, the boundaries between reality and fantasy are extremely flexible. On the other hand, some very simple form of classification may be of value in order to make it easier for the adult reader to find books or authors he or she requires, and as a starting point for matching text to readers.

For these reasons the reviews are divided into four sections, in terms of the approximate level of reading development of the child. Such classifications should obviously be treated as only the most approximate of guides, since individual children's interests and reading competence varies so much. The divisions used here are really only for convenience, and many authors and books could be classified differently with equal logic (books like Jan Pienkowski's

Christmas or the work of Maurice Sendak could have been included in any of the four sections!). And, of course, authors often write books suitable for different age groups. However, it may be that some classification, even if imperfect, is better than none, and in addition the suggestions made in Appendix 2 (pp. 133–40) of picture books as appropriate starting points for work on particular topics may be helpful.

Reviews of Picture Books

The reviews are intended to be of use to adults, particularly teachers, working with children of primary school age: that is, four or five to eleven or thereabouts.

The name of the illustrator is indicated in brackets after the author's name (when it is possible to distinguish him or her). Each recommended title is followed by the name of the publisher(s) – generally hardback followed by paperback, but in cases of ambiguity (H) or (P) are used to indicate the type. In many cases only a selection of an author's output is referred to, as in the cases of the prolific Dick Bruna and Brian Wildsmith; other equally good books by the same author may be as or more easily available.

Books go in and out of print at great speed, and so it is quite possible that by the time this is read a particular text may no longer be available. Books that are known to be out of print at the time of writing (June 1990) have with a few exceptions been omitted; those that remain should be easily available from public libraries. No prices are given as these also change rapidly and inexorably, but as a rough guide hardback picture books at present generally cost £5–£8, while paperback versions are usually priced between £1.50 and £3.00, although there are exceptions in each case, and in each direction.

The books included are all well worth consideration, but an asterisk (*) has been appended to those titles that are especially noteworthy. All the books are illustrated in full colour except those indicated by (B & W), i.e. black and white.

A large number of reviews are included in the following pages, and teachers and others who have not used picture books much before may therefore find some indication of starting points useful. In Appendix 1 (pp. 131–32), therefore, a few outstanding books are recommended, and teachers may wish to consider them for use as the initial core of a classroom collection.

The intention, and hope, is that all these brief reviews will introduce teachers (and children) to at least some good books of which they were not aware before; and that they will be encouraged to explore even further.

Notes and References

1. Such as the Fontana Children's Catalogue, from Fontana Paperbacks, 8 Grafton Street, London W1X 3LA.

2. *Children's Fiction Stocklist*, the Holt-Jackson Book Co. Ltd, Preston Road, Lytham, Lancashire FY8 5AX; *Children's Paperback Directory*, Books for Students, Bird Road, Heathcote, Warwick CV34 6TB.

3. Available from the Centre for Language in Primary Education, Webber Row Teachers' Centre, Webber Row, London SE1 8QW.

4. Available from the Children's Literature Association of Ireland, Church of Ireland College of Education, 96 Upper Rathmines Road, Dublin 6.

5. Available from the SE Essex Teacher's Centre, Hadleigh, Essex.

6. Available from the School Bookshop Association, 1 Effingham Road, Lee, London SE12 8NZ.

7. Contact Geoff Fox, School of Education, University of Exeter, Exeter EX4 4QJ. See also the specialist journal *Signal*, from The Thimble Press, Lockwood, Station Road, South Woodchester, Glos GL5 5EQ.

8. Waterland, L., *Read With Me* (2nd edn), Stroud, Thimble Press, 1988, p. 41.

9. For an excellent guide to all aspects of poetry, see Styles, M. and Triggs, P., *Poetry 0−16*, available from Books for Keeps, 1 Effingham Road, Lee, London SE12 8NZ.

10. Warlow, A., 'Alternative worlds available', in Meek, M. *et al.* (eds.), *The Cool Web: The Pattern of Children's Reading*, London, Bodley Head, 1977.

11. *Ibid.*, p. 100.

Picture Books Mentioned in the Text

Pienkowski, J., *Christmas*, Heinemann/Picture Puffin.

8
PICTURE BOOKS FOR BEGINNING READING

(In these lists, H stands for hardback, P for paperback).

AHLBERG, JANET AND ALLAN
* EACH PEACH PEAR PLUM Viking Kestrel/Picture Lion
'Each peach pear plum I spy Tom Thumb' – and there in the picture he is, if you look very carefully. A delightful story, a cleverly conceived game of I-spy, and, as in all the very best picture books, the words and the pictures are interdependent. An excellent picture book.
* THE BABY'S CATALOGUE Viking Kestrel/Picture Puffin
As many a parent has noticed, young children are fascinated by catalogues – the interesting objects and the bright colours are irresistible. So the Ahlbergs have produced a wonderful catalogue of their own, centred around babies and their lives – breakfasts, toys, games, nappies of course, pets, a hilarious page of 'accidents', and so on. A book for all children, and all Mums and Dads!
By the same author (Allan Ahlberg): the Red Nose Reader series, such as TELL US A STORY Walker (H & P); ONE, TWO, FLEA Walker (H & P); and others.

ALBOROUGH, JEZ
BARE BEAR Picture Knight (P)
A very funny story of a polar bear getting undressed for a shower and exposing his big bare bear behind!
In the same series: RUNNING BEAR Black (H); CUPBOARD BEAR Walker (H).
By the same author: THE GRASS IS GREENER Black/Picturemac; ESTHER'S TRUNK Walker (H).

BAKER, ALAN
* BENJAMIN'S BOOK Deutsch (H)
A mouse accidentally leaves a small paw print on the nice clean page of the

book. His attempts to remove the smudge result in a total mess of the entire page (a very common experience for children!), so he sadly tears the whole page out and throws it away. 'I do like to leave things as I find them,' he says, not noticing that he has left a small paw print on the next page of the book! A delightful joke shared between author and reader.

In the same series: BENJAMIN AND THE BOX Deutsch (H); BENJAMIN'S DREADFUL DREAM Deutsch (H); BENJAMIN'S PORTRAIT Deutsch/ Picture Corgi.

BANG, MOLLY
TEN, NINE, EIGHT Julia MacRae/Picture Puffin
An attractive counting book about a girl going to bed: from 'ten small toes all washed and warm' to 'one big girl all ready for bed'. Useful for early counting experiences.

BERENSTAIN, STAN AND JAN
BEARS IN THE NIGHT Collins (H & P)
The little bears enjoy sneaking out at night to explore — until they come face to face with something very frightening! A good example of a very simple text for beginning readers, which is suitably repetitious without being dull and boring.

In the same series: BEARS' HOLIDAY Collins (H & P); HE BEAR SHE BEAR Collins (H & P); BEARS ON WHEELS Collins (H & P); and many others.

By the same authors: INSIDE OUTSIDE UPSIDE DOWN Collins (H & P); OLD HAT, NEW HAT Collins (H & P); and many others.

BRACKEN, CAROLYN
LITTLE BO PEEP AND OTHER NURSERY RHYMES Ladybird (H)
One of four hardback books which between them contain most of the common nursery rhymes. As always with Ladybird, good value for money.

In the same series: LITTLE MISS MUFFET AND OTHER NURSERY RHYMES Ladybird (H); LITTLE TOMMY TUCKER AND OTHER NURSERY RHYMES Ladybird (H); LITTLE JACK HORNER AND OTHER NURSERY RHYMES Ladybird (H).

BRIGGS, RAYMOND
THE FAIRY TALE TREASURY Picture Puffin (P)
A comprehensive collection of fairy tales, attractively illustrated. Excellent stories for reading or telling to children.

By the same author: THE MOTHER GOOSE TREASURY (out of print).

BROWN, RUTH
A DARK DARK TALE Andersen/Hippo
The well-known repetitive and cumulative story, with appropriately dark illustrations and a neat ending. Very useful for beginning readers.
By the same author: LADYBIRD, LADYBIRD Beaver (P).

BRUNA, DICK
I AM A CLOWN Methuen (H)
Simple caricature pictures of a little boy dressed up for different occupations, with an appropriate label (doctor, farmer, fireman, etc.). Opinions tend to be divided about Dick Bruna: his books are popular with very young children, but do seem a bit limited in the scope they provide for discussion. And does a book like this reinforce the idea that certain occupations are appropriate for boys, while others (like nursing and teaching which are not included here) are for girls?
By the same author: THE APPLE Methuen (H); THE EGG Methuen (H); THE CIRCUS Methuen (H); I CAN READ Methuen (H); THE KING Methuen (H); THE LITTLE BIRD Methuen (H); the Miffy series, Methuen (H); and many others.

BUCKNALL, CAROLINE
ONE BEAR ALL ALONE Macmillan/Picturemac
A lively counting book following some bears on an outing. Clear and uncluttered pictures.
In the same series: ONE BEAR IN THE PICTURE Macmillan/Picturemac.

BURNINGHAM, JOHN
ALPHABET BOOK Walker (H & P)
Attractive and often funny pictures of a little boy involved with an object or animal for each letter of the alphabet. Very distinctive illustrations.
In the same series: OPPOSITES BOOK Walker (H & P); NUMBERS BOOK Walker (H & P); COLOURS BOOK Walker (H & P).
By the same author: SEASONS Cape (H).

CAMPBELL, ROD
* DEAR ZOO Campbell Blackie/Picture Puffin
'I wrote to the zoo to send me a pet. They sent me a . . .' Lift up the flap on each page to find various unsuitable animals, until the last page reveals a little puppy. A delightful book for small children, and one in which anticipation and prediction carry the reader along.

By the same author: MY DAY Collins/Picture Lion; OH DEAR! Campbell
Blackie/Picture Piper; ABC Blackie (H).

CARLE, ERIC
* THE VERY HUNGRY CATERPILLAR Hamish Hamilton/Picture Puffin
A small and hungry caterpillar eats through an amazing variety of food (and
through the pages of the book!). Now no longer small he builds himself a cocoon
and emerges as a beautiful butterfly. A most attractive and exciting book for
children — they love following the progress of the caterpillar through the pages!
THE BAD TEMPERED LADYBIRD Hamish Hamilton/Picture Puffin
The bad tempered ladybird is apparently always ready for a fight with any of the
animals it meets, but tends to back off fast when it comes to it! A book which
makes innovative use of different sizes of page and different sizes of print.
By the same author: THE VERY BUSY SPIDER Hamish Hamilton (H); THE
MIXED UP CHAMELEON Hamish Hamilton/Picture Puffin; THE SECRET
BIRTHDAY MESSAGE Picturemac (P).

CARLSON, NANCY
HARRIET'S RECITAL Picture Puffin (P)
Harriet loves dancing but is very nervous in the week leading up to the class's
recital. Needless to say, all goes well on the night. A simple story about
overcoming one's fears.
By the same author: LOUDMOUTH GEORGE AND THE BIG RACE Dent/
Picture Corgi; LOUDMOUTH GEORGE AND THE FISHING TRIP Dent/
Picture Corgi.

COLLINGTON, PETER
LITTLE PICKLE Methuen/Magnet
A naughty little girl dreams that Mum falls asleep in the pushchair. Meanwhile,
the little girl sets off for wild adventures at sea, eventually to be rescued from the
storm by fishermen. No words, but the story line is strong and clear.
By the same author: THE ANGEL AND THE SOLDIER BOY Methuen/
Magnet.

CROWTHER, ROBERT
THE MOST AMAZING HIDE-AND-SEEK COUNTING BOOK Viking
Kestrel (H)
A pop-up book in which each number from one to twenty, and then in tens to a
hundred, is appealingly illustrated. Mechanically very ingenious. Popular with
children, but like many pop-up books easily damaged in normal (i.e. rough and
careless!) use.

In the same series: THE MOST AMAZING HIDE-AND-SEEK ALPHABET BOOK Viking Kestrel (H); THE MOST AMAZING HIDE-AND-SEEK OPPOSITES BOOK Viking Kestrel (H).

GALDONE, PAUL
OVER IN THE MEADOW Macdonald (H)
The old nursery counting rhyme, with lively illustrations.
By the same author: CINDERELLA World's Work (H); THE THREE BLIND MICE Heinemann (H); THE THREE LITTLE KITTENS Heinemann (H).

GARLAND, SARAH
HAVING A PICNIC Bodley Head/Picture Puffin
Mum takes toddler and baby out for what appears to be a rather chilly picnic. Few words, plenty to talk about in the pictures.
In the same series: DOING THE WASHING Bodley Head/Picture Puffin; GOING SHOPPING Bodley Head/Picture Puffin; COMING TO TEA Bodley Head/Picture Puffin.

GINSBURG, MIRRA (Tafuri, Nancy)
ACROSS THE STREAM Julia MacRae/Picture Puffin
A hen and three chicks escape across the stream and away from a fox by getting a lift on the backs of a duck and three ducklings. Very simple rhyming text, huge bold pictures.
By the same author: FOUR BRAVE SAILORS Julia MacRae/Walker; WHERE DOES THE SUN GO AT NIGHT? Walker (P).

GRETZ, SUSANNA
* THE BEARS WHO WENT TO THE SEASIDE Black/Picture Puffin (P)
Five bears − and a dog − each with his own distinct personality, spend two generally happy days on the beach. A funny and quirky book, from a useful series.
In the same series: THE BEARS WHO STAYED INDOORS Black/Picture Puffin; TEDDY BEARS 1 TO 10 Picture Lion (P); TEDDY BEARS ABC Black/Picture Lion; TEDDYBEARS' MOVING DAY Black/Hippo; TEDDYBEARS GO SHOPPING Black/Hippo; ROGER TAKES CHARGE Bodley Head/Picture Lion; and others.

HILL, ERIC
* WHERE'S SPOT? Heinemann/Picture Puffin
Spot's Mum searches the house for her errant son. On each page a lift up flap discloses an assortment of other animals ('Is he under the bed?' No, it's a

crocodile!) until Spot is eventually discovered in a basket. Deceptively simple, excellent for prediction, very effective.

In the same series: SPOT'S FIRST WALK Heinemann/Picture Puffin; SPOT'S BIRTHDAY PARTY Heinemann/Picture Puffin; SPOT'S FIRST CHRISTMAS Heinemann/Picture Puffin; SPOT GOES TO SCHOOL Heinemann/Picture Puffin; SPOT GOES ON HOLIDAY Heinemann/Picture Puffin; SPOT GOES TO THE CIRCUS Heinemann/Picture Puffin; and others.

HUTCHINS, PAT

* ROSIE'S WALK Bodley Head/Picture Puffin

Rosie the hen goes for a walk in the country and eventually gets back home in time for dinner. But Rosie does not seem to be aware, and it is certainly never mentioned in the 32-word text, that a fox is just about to strike. Luckily (or is Rosie less oblivious than she seems?) disasters befall him at every attempt. A modern classic: the words and the pictures work together beautifully (see also pp. 17–20).

* GOODNIGHT, OWL! Bodley Head/Picture Puffin

Owl tries to sleep but is kept awake by all the other animals. Not until night falls does he get his revenge, as his screeching wakes everyone up! Very simple, very repetitive and quite beautiful. A firm favourite with young children, and excellent for simple dramatization.

By the same author: THE SURPRISE PARTY Bodley Head/Picture Puffin; ONE EYED JAKE Bodley Head/Picture Puffin; CLOCKS AND MORE CLOCKS Bodley Head/Picture Puffin; 1 HUNTER Picture Puffin (P); THE WIND BLEW Bodley Head/Picture Puffin; TOM AND SAM Bodley Head/Picture Puffin; THE VERY WORST MONSTER Bodley Head/Picture Puffin; CHANGES, CHANGES Bodley Head (H); THE DOORBELL RANG Bodley Head/Picture Puffin; DON'T FORGET THE BACON Bodley Head/Picture Puffin; and others.

ISADORA, RACHEL

I SEE Julia MacRae/Picture Lion

Pictures of interesting objects a small child can see. Few words, plenty to discuss; beautifully illustrated.

In the same series: I TOUCH Picture Lion (P); I HEAR Julia MacRae/Picture Lion.

LIONNI, LEO

LITTLE BLUE AND LITTLE YELLOW Hodder (H)

When blue and yellow hug each other they become green, and are unrecognized by their respective families. Fortunately they disentangle themselves, and are welcomed back. An utterly simple, but very effective introduction to colours and their constituents.

By the same author: FISH IS FISH Picture Puffin (P); CORNELIUS Andersen (H); IT'S MINE! Andersen/Picture Knight.

LLOYD, DAVID (Voake, Charlotte)
OVER THE MOON: A BOOK OF NURSERY RHYMES Walker (H & P)
All the best known nursery rhymes, attractively illustrated. A useful collection.

MARIS, RON
IS ANYONE HOME? Julia MacRae/Picture Puffin
Lift the flap to find interesting people and animals behind every door in the farmyard. Cleverly designed and very effective.

By the same author: ARE YOU THERE, BEAR? Julia MacRae/Picture Puffin; BETTER MOVE ON, FROG! Julia MacRae/Picture Lion; THE PUNCH AND JUDY BOOK Gollancz/Picture Lion; I WISH I COULD FLY Julia MacRae/Picture Puffin; MY BOOK Julia MacRae/Picture Puffin; HOLD TIGHT, BEAR Julia MacRae/Walker.

McKEE, DAVID
* NOT NOW, BERNARD Andersen/Sparrow
The delightful story of Bernard's attempts to attract his parents' attention. But whatever happens, even when he is eaten by a monster, his Mum and Dad just carry on saying, 'Not now, Bernard'!

NICOLL, HELEN (Pienkowski, Jan)
* MEG AND MOG Heinemann/Picture Puffin
Meg the witch, Mog her cat, and Owl go off to a party with the other witches. Unfortunately, Meg's spell goes wrong (as often seems to happen in this series!) and the other witches are all turned into mice. Bright primary colours and very imaginative use of text in cartoon-style 'bubbles'.

In the same series: MEG'S EGGS Heinemann/Picture Puffin; MEG'S VEG Heinemann/Picture Puffin; MOG AT THE ZOO Heinemann/Picture Puffin; MEG AT SEA Heinemann/Picture Puffin; MEG ON THE MOON Heinemann/Picture Puffin; MOG IN THE FOG Heinemann/Picture Puffin; and many others.

ORMEROD, JAN
* SUNSHINE Picture Puffin (P)
A small girl wakes up early, but Dad lies on in bed immersed in his newspaper and Mum goes back to sleep. The little girl gets washed and dressed, but when

she looks at the clock she realizes how late it is, and Mum and Dad have to rush about in a panic to get ready in time to go out to work. A lovely book without words, uncomfortably reminiscent of many a morning! Highly recommended (see also pp. 14–17).
In the same series: MOONLIGHT Viking Kestrel/Picture Puffin.
By the same author: BE BRAVE BILLY Dent (H).

PIENKOWSKI, JAN
NUMBERS Heinemann/Picture Puffin
A very simple counting book, with bright, clear and simple pictures. One of a very useful series of information books for very young children.
In the same series: ABC Heinemann/Picture Puffin; COLOURS Heinemann/Picture Puffin; HOMES Heinemann/Picture Puffin; SHAPES Heinemann/Picture Puffin; SIZES Heinemann/Picture Puffin; TIME Heinemann/Picture Puffin; WEATHER Heinemann/Picture Puffin; ZOO Heinemann/Picture Puffin.

POMERANTZ, CHARLOTTE (Aruego, Jose and Dewey, Ariane)
ONE DUCK, ANOTHER DUCK Picture Puffin (P)
A story of Danny the owl's attempts to count the ducks and swans at the pond. He gets it right eventually, with a little help from grandmother. Most expressive pictures, useful for children just learning to count.
By the same author: ALL ASLEEP Julia MacRae (H).

ROFFEY, MAUREEN
LOOK, THERE'S MY HAT! Bodley Head/Piccolo
Clever hole-in-the-page illustrations of a little girl appropriating the belongings of other members of her family! Very simple text.
By the same author: HOME SWEET HOME Bodley Head/Piccolo.

SCARRY, RICHARD
* RICHARD SCARRY'S BEST WORD BOOK EVER Hamlyn (H)
Tremendously popular with children, Richard Scarry's books gain their strength from their colourful and detailed anthropomorphic illustrations. This is a good example, containing pictures of just about every conceivable object children might be interested in, with endless opportunities for discussion. The text is rather vestigial, but in this case it is a relatively minor drawback. Good value.
* RICHARD SCARRY'S BEST NURSERY RHYMES EVER Hamlyn (H)
In my experience the most popular book of nursery rhymes. Huge, bold, colourful and funny pictures of animals, and big print.
By the same author: BEST STORY BOOK EVER Hamlyn (H); GREAT BIG

SCHOOLHOUSE Collins (H); CARS AND TRUCKS AND THINGS THAT GO Collins (H); and many others.

SEUSS, DR
THE CAT IN THE HAT Collins (H & P)
Lively doggerel, repetitious but rhythmical, and a real story to keep children interested and turning the pages. One of an excellent and well-known series enjoyed by several generations of young readers. Absurd but appropriate pictures, and well worth consideration.
In the same series: THE CAT IN THE HAT COMES BACK! Collins (H & P); GREEN EGGS AND HAM Collins (H & P); ONE FISH TWO FISH RED FISH BLUE FISH Collins (H & P); and many others.

STOBBS, WILLIAM
THIS LITTLE PIGGY Bodley Head (H)
The traditional finger counting rhyme with lively illustrations. Very useful for early readers.
By the same author: OLD MACDONALD HAD A FARM Oxford (H); THE HOUSE THAT JACK BUILT Oxford (H); THERE'S A HOLE IN MY BUCKET Oxford (H).

TAFURI, NANCY
WHO'S COUNTING Picture Puffin (P)
A simple counting book; big, clear and unfussy pictures.
By the same author: HAVE YOU SEEN MY DUCKLING? Picture Puffin (P); EARLY MORNING IN THE BARN Picture Puffin (P); DO NOT DISTURB Julia MacRae (H).

VIPONT, ELFRIDA (Briggs, Raymond)
THE ELEPHANT AND THE BAD BABY Hamish Hamilton/Picture Puffin
The elephant takes all sorts of goodies from various shops, but he gets fed up when the baby never ever says 'please'. (The shopkeepers, who chase after the delinquent baby and elephant, are none too happy either!) Luckily, the bad baby's Mum is ready and willing to give them all pancakes for tea. Repetitious words, and very appropriate illustrations.

WATANABE, SHIGEO (Ohtomo, Yasuo)
* HOW DO I PUT IT ON? Bodley Head/Picture Puffin
A little bear gets in a muddle with his clothes, trying to fit his shoes on to his ears and so on; but he eventually gets everything in the right place. One of an excellent series for very young children.

In the same series: HALLO! HOW ARE YOU? Bodley Head/Picture Puffin; I CAN DO IT! Picture Puffin (P); HOW DO I EAT IT? Picture Puffin (P); I'M THE KING OF THE CASTLE Picture Puffin (P); READY STEADY GO! Bodley Head (H); I'M HAVING A BATH WITH PAPA Bodley Head/Picture Puffin; I'M PLAYING WITH PAPA Bodley Head (H).

WELLS, ROSEMARY
MAX'S NEW SUIT Collins (H)
Max the baby rabbit hates his new suit so much that he resists help in dressing from his sister Ruby, and puts on all the clothes upside down! A series of very simple stories which very young children enjoy.
In the same series: MAX'S RIDE Collins (H); MAX'S FIRST WORD Collins (H); MAX'S TOYS Collins (H); MAX'S CHOCOLATE CHICKEN Collins (H); and others.
By the same author: SHY CHARLES Collins (H).

WILDSMITH, BRIAN
ABC Oxford University Press (H & P)
Vibrant colour in the paintings, mainly of animals, including some unusual ones such as iguana, unicorn and jaguar. The names are written in upper- and lower-case letters, and in different colours. Plenty to discuss!
By the same author: CAT ON THE MAT Oxford (P); THE TRUNK Oxford (P); THE NEST Oxford (P); THE TWELVE DAYS OF CHRISTMAS Oxford (P); THE CIRCUS Oxford (H & P); and many others.

ZACHARIAS, THOMAS AND WANDA
BUT WHERE IS THE GREEN PARROT? Bodley Head/Picture Piper
A detailed picture on each page (a train, a house, a garden), in which the green parrot can be found hiding if the child is observant!

ZIEFERT, HARRIET (Brown, Richard)
NICKY'S NOISY NIGHT Picture Puffin (P)
Nicky the kitten cannot get to sleep until she has investigated all the strange noises in the house. A worthwhile little lift-the-flap story, much the same level as the Spot books.
In the same series: NICKY'S PICNIC Picture Puffin (P); THANK YOU, NICKY! Picture Puffin (P).
By the same author: WHERE'S MY EASTER EGG? Picture Puffin (P); DON'T CRY, BABY SAM Picture Lion (P).

9
PICTURE BOOKS FOR DEVELOPING READING

AHLBERG, JANET AND ALLAN
* PEEPO! Viking Kestrel/Picture Puffin
A delightful and innovative book; a day in the life of a wartime family, seen through (almost literally!) the eyes of a baby. The pictures are nostalgic and evocative, the text simple and rhythmical. Lots to look at, lots to talk about.
* BURGLAR BILL Heinemann/Little Mammoth
Burglar Bill gets more than he bargained for when he steals a box, for inside is a baby! Bill attempts to change baby's nappy and feed him on toast and marmalade and cups of tea, and life gets even more complicated when he is himself burgled by a lady burglar! Hilarious; children love the story.
By the same authors: FUNNYBONES Heinemann/Picture Lion.

ALLEN, PAMELA
WHO SANK THE BOAT? Hamish Hamilton (H & P)
The cow, donkey, sheep and pig all manage to get into the boat without sinking it, but the tiny mouse's weight is just too much for safety! Most expressive pictures and rhythmical text.
By the same author: HERBERT AND HARRY Hamish Hamilton (H); A LION IN THE NIGHT Hamish Hamilton (H); MR ARCHIMEDES' BATH Hamish Hamilton (H); MR MCGEE Hamish Hamilton/Picture Puffin; BERTIE AND THE BEAR Hamish Hamilton/Picture Puffin.

ANNO, MITSUMASO
ANNO'S COUNTING BOOK Picturemac (P)
A pastoral scene changes on successive pages, through the day and through the year. The pictures also gradually fill up from the number 0, a harsh and empty landscape, to the busy community of number 12, with its dozen houses, people,

trees, reindeer and much else. As usual with this innovative artist, a simple idea cleverly executed. Some of Anno's best books are now sadly out of print, but the following are still available.
By the same author: ANNO'S ITALY Bodley Head (H); ANNO'S FACES Reinhardt (H); ANNO'S FLEA MARKET Bodley Head (H); ANNO'S PEEKABOO Bodley Head (H).

ASCH, FRANK
* JUST LIKE DADDY Carousel (P)
A little bear gets up, dressed and out fishing, all just like Daddy does. But when he catches a big fish, it is much more like Mummy's! A good example of a very simple and repetitive story, with just the tiny little twist at the end to make it interesting.
By the same author: HAPPY BIRTHDAY MOON Picture Corgi (P); MOON CAKE Picture Corgi (P); SKYFIRE Hodder/Picture Corgi; GOODBYE HOUSE Hodder & Stoughton/Picture Corgi.

BAUM, LOUIS (Bouma, Paddy)
* ARE WE NEARLY THERE? Bodley Head/Magnet
After a day in the park, Dad takes his son home on the train. 'Are we nearly there?' asks the little boy, eagerly anticipating reunion with Mum. But after returning the little boy, Dad does not stay and waves goodbye outside the house. A reassuring read for children, but very sad for adults!
By the same author: AFTER DARK Andersen (H); I WANT TO SEE THE MOON Bodley Head/Magnet; JUJU AND THE PIRATE Andersen/Magnet.

BILLAM, ROSEMARY (Julian-Ottie, Vanessa)
ALPACA Collins/Picture Lion
Alpaca the toy rabbit is feeling a bit neglected now that Ellen has a new owl and doll to play with. But as he discovers, he is really still Ellen's favourite. A gentle and reassuring story about friendship.
In the same series: ALPACA IN THE PARK Collins/Picture Lion; COME ON, ALPACA Collins/Picture Lion.

BLAKE, QUENTIN
* MR MAGNOLIA Cape/Picture Lion
Poor Mr Magnolia has many things, but unfortunately only one boot — until the end of this crazy and delightfully illustrated verse. Great fun.
By the same author: THE STORY OF THE DANCING FROG Picture Lion (P).

BRADMAN, TONY AND BROWNE, EILEEN
THROUGH MY WINDOW Methuen/Little Mammoth
Jo is ill and watches events in the street from her window, until Mum returns from work, bringing with her a nice surprise. Everyday urban life in a simple and easily read story.
In the same series: IN A MINUTE Methuen (H); WAIT AND SEE Methuen (H).
By the same author (Tony Bradman): THE SANDAL Andersen (H); and others.

BRANDENBURG, FRANZ (Aliki)
AUNT NINA AND HER NEPHEWS AND NIECES (out of print)
Six nephews and nieces visit Aunt Nina on Fluffy the cat's birthday, but they cannot find the latter anywhere. When they eventually do, they discover that it is the birthday of six tiny kittens too.
In the same series: AUNT NINA'S VISIT Piccolo (P); AUNT NINA, GOOD-NIGHT Bodley Head (H).
By the same author: I DON'T FEEL WELL Picture Puffin (P).

BREINBURG, PETRONELLA (Lloyd, Errol)
MY BROTHER SEAN Picture Puffin (P)
Sean's first day at school is distressing, but ends with a kind of resolution, as Sean smiles 'a teeny weeny smile'. An unusual picture book, and a valuable portrayal of a black child's first experience of school.

BRIGGS, RAYMOND
* THE SNOWMAN Hamish Hamilton/Picture Puffin
A little boy makes a snowman who comes to life in the night. After exploring the boy's house, they fly off together, before returning as the sun rises. Next morning, the little boy sadly finds that the snowman has melted away. No words, but beautifully illustrated and most appealing. A picture book for all ages. An excellent video version is available from Weston Woods.

BROWN, MARC
WITCHES FOUR Hamish Hamilton/Picture Corgi
A simple and repetitive story in verse about four daft witches. Lively illustrations and good fun.
By the same author: THERE'S NO PLACE LIKE HOME Collins (H); ARTHUR'S TOOTH Piccadilly/Picture Corgi; ARTHUR'S BABY Piccadilly (H); and others.

BURNINGHAM, JOHN
* MR GUMPY'S OUTING Cape/Picture Puffin
Mr Gumpy and an assortment of children and animals go for a peaceful ride in a boat – until they start to misbehave and the inevitable happens. However, when they've dried themselves in the sun they all walk home for a magnificent tea. The repetitive yet rhythmical language and the superbly appropriate illustrations make this a firm favourite with young children.
In the same series: MR GUMPY'S MOTOR CAR Cape/Picture Puffin.
* THE SHOPPING BASKET Cape/Picture Lion
Mum is a bit cross with Steven when it takes him ages to get a few groceries from the corner shop. But what she does not realize is that on the way he has been confronted by a bear, a monkey, a kangaroo, a goat, a pig and an elephant, each of which he has had to outwit before proceeding on his way. A clever and amusing book.
By the same author: TRUBLOFF Cape/Piper; CANNONBALL SIMP Cape (H); BORKA Cape/Picture Puffin; WHERE'S JULIUS? Cape/Picture Piper; JOHN PATRICK NORMAN McHENNESSY – THE BOY WHO WAS ALWAYS LATE Cape (H); OI! GET OFF MY TRAIN Cape (H); and others.

DE PAOLA, TOMIE
* THE CHRISTMAS PAGEANT Picture Lion (P)
The familiar words of the Christmas story illustrated by scenes from a children's pageant. Deft and amusing pictures.
By the same author: THE MAGIC PASTA POT Andersen (H); BOB AND BOBBY Pocket Puffin (P); NANA UPSTAIRS AND NANA DOWNSTAIRS Methuen (H); THE CLOWN OF GOD Magnet (P).

DODD, LYNLEY
* HAIRY MACLARY FROM DONALDSON'S DAIRY Spindlewood/ Picture Puffin
Hairy Maclary and an odd assortment of other canines walk through the town – until they meet Scarface Claw, the toughest Tom in town. Enough to make any dog turn tail! A rhythmical and humorous story.
In the same series: HAIRY MACLARY'S BONE Spindlewood/Picture Puffin; HAIRY MACLARY SCATTERCAT Spindlewood/Picture Puffin; HAIRY MACLARY'S CATERWAUL CAPER Spindlewood/Picture Puffin; and others.
By the same author: WAKE UP BEAR Spindlewood/Picture Puffin.

DUVOISIN, ROGER
* SEE WHAT I AM (out of print)

A lovely book about the three primary colours and how, together with black and white, they can combine to make beautiful colour pictures.

FALCONER, ELIZABETH
LITTLE GNOME Orchard/Picture Lion
Little gnome visits his two uncles and spends a happy day with them. Gentle little story, attractively illustrated.
By the same author: THREE LITTLE WITCHES Orchard/Picture Lion.

FRENCH, FIONA
RISE, SHINE! Methuen (H)
A traditional spiritual based on the story of 'Noah's Ark', with dramatic and very effective illustrations.
By the same author: CINDERELLA Oxford (H); HUNT THE THIMBLE Oxford (H); MAID OF THE WOOD Oxford (H); SNOW WHITE IN NEW YORK Oxford (H & P).

GOODALL, JOHN S.
* PADDY PORK'S HOLIDAY Macmillan (H)
Inquisitive Paddy sets out for a relaxing rambling holiday, but gets more than he bargained for when after a series of hair-raising and hilarious escapades he is mistaken for a famous concert pianist. A cleverly constructed book in which alternate pages and half pages carry the story without any need for words. Plenty to talk about.
In the same series: THE ADVENTURES OF PADDY PORK Macmillan (H); PADDY'S EVENING OUT Macmillan/Picturemac.
By the same author: SHREWBETTINA'S BIRTHDAY Picturemac (P); THE MIDNIGHT ADVENTURES OF KELLY, DOT AND ESMERALDA Picturemac (P); THE SURPRISE PICNIC Macmillan/Picturemac.

GORDON, MARGARET
THE SUPERMARKET MICE Viking Kestrel/Picture Puffin
The mice are happily settled in the supermarket − plenty to eat for everyone − until a cat is brought in to deal with them. Luckily he is a rather dopey creature and they are certainly very resourceful mice. An amusing story, well illustrated and useful for discussion.
By the same author: WILBERFORCE GOES ON A PICNIC Viking Kestrel/ Picture Puffin; WILBERFORCE GOES SHOPPING Viking Kestrel/Picture Puffin; WILBERFORCE GOES TO A PARTY Viking Kestrel/Picture Puffin; FROG'S HOLIDAY Viking Kestrel/Picture Puffin.

HAWKINS, COLIN AND JACQUI
MAX AND THE MAGIC WORD Viking Kestrel/Picture Puffin
Max the bear asks his friends for a share of their ice-cream and cake, but no one will give him any because he never remembers to say the magic word. What, wonders Max, could the word possibly be? (It is 'please', of course, and not as one group of children insisted, 'abracadabra'!)
By the same authors: JEN THE HEN Piccadilly/Picture Puffin; TOG THE DOG Piccadilly/Picture Puffin; PAT THE CAT Picture Puffin (P); WHAT'S THE TIME MR WOLF? Heinemann/Picture Lion; THE GRANNY BOOK Picture Lion (P); MR WOLF'S WEEK Heinemann/Picture Lion; and others.

HAYES, SARAH (Craig, Helen)
THIS IS THE BEAR Walker (H & P)
A rhythmical story of a bear who gets lost and a little boy who searches and eventually finds him. Rather reminiscent of 'The House that Jack Built', but has a charm of its own.
In the same series: THIS IS THE BEAR AND THE PICNIC LUNCH Walker (H & P).
By the same author: HAPPY CHRISTMAS, GEMMA Walker (P); EAT UP, GEMMA Walker (P).

HOFF, SYD
* STANLEY Heinemann (P)
Stanley is an unusual caveman who much prefers growing flowers and painting pictures to whacking people with clubs. Rejected and isolated as an unnatural softy, Stanley has to leave his cave and, finding the open fields uncomfortable places to live, proceeds to invent the first house. 'Caves are old-fashioned' he suggests to the others, who are much impressed! A funny story with a point, told in simple language, with large and appropriately amusing illustrations.
By the same author: DANNY AND THE DINOSAUR World's Work/Young Puffin; GRIZZWOLD World's Work/Young Puffin; JULIUS World's Work (H).

HOWE, JAMES (Hoban, Lilian)
THE DAY THE TEACHER WENT BANANAS Viking Kestrel/Picture Puffin
A rather unusual teacher turns up to school: one who grunts and eats sixteen bananas for lunch! A cheerful and zany little story.

HUGHES, SHIRLEY
LUCY AND TOM'S ABC Gollancz/Picture Puffin

Humorous little stories about Lucy and Tom centred around everyday objects – dogs, houses, streets, toys – through the alphabet. Lots of topics for discussion, but some of the text would be difficult for a child to read alone.
In the same series: LUCY AND TOM AT THE SEASIDE Gollancz/Corgi; LUCY AND TOM'S CHRISTMAS Gollancz/Picture Puffin; LUCY AND TOM'S DAY Gollancz/Picture Puffin; LUCY AND TOM GO TO SCHOOL Gollancz/Carousel.

KELLER, HOLLY
FRANCIE'S DAY IN BED Julia MacRae/Hippo
It is strange to lie in bed when you are not feeling too good, and hear all the everyday sounds of people going to work, Mum doing the housework and so on. Fortunately Francie is sufficiently recovered by tea time to anticipate a cupcake! Well-produced book, simple text, attractive illustrations.
By the same author: TOO BIG Hippo (P); GERALDINE'S BLANKET Hippo (P); TWO SLEEPY SHEEP Hippo (P).

KENT, JACK
CLOTILDA'S MAGIC (out of print)
'Nobody wants a fairy godmother nowadays,' says Clotilda, feeling very sorry for herself. But as Tommy and Betty soon discover, fairy godmothers still have their uses. A witty little story, with nicely absurd illustrations.
By the same author: THERE'S NO SUCH THING AS A DRAGON Blackie (H & P); THE FAT CAT Picture Puffin (P).

KURATOMI, CHIZUKO (Kakimoto, Kozo)
* MR BEAR, SHIPWRECKED Macdonald (H)
Mr Bear is a large, lovable, but rather stupid bear who stumbles into adventures. Here he is shipwrecked on an island inhabited by rabbits, who are at first rather suspicious of him. A popular, beautifully produced and wonderfully illustrated series.
In the same series: MR BEAR GOES TO SEA Macdonald (H); MR BEAR IN THE AIR Macdonald (P); MR BEAR POSTMAN Macdonald (P); MR BEAR'S MEAL Macdonald (P); MR BEAR STATION-MASTER Macdonald (P); MR BEAR'S TRUMPET Macdonald (H & P); REMEMBER MR BEAR Macdonald (P); MR BEAR'S BIRTHDAY Macmillan (H).

LOBEL, ARNOLD
* FROG AND TOAD TOGETHER World's Work/Young Puffin
Short, gentle little fables about the adventures of two friends. For example, Toad loses the list on which he has written down his tasks for the day. Without it

he forgets that the only remaining item is 'Go To Sleep'. Excellent easy reading and meaningful stories.
In the same series: DAYS WITH FROG AND TOAD World's Work/Young Puffin; FROG AND TOAD ALL YEAR World's Work/Young Puffin.
By the same author: MOUSE TALES Young Puffin (P); OWL AT HOME World's Work (P).

McKEE, DAVID
* KING ROLLO AND THE TREE Andersen (H)
King Rollo is determined to climb to the top of the tree, in spite of all the warnings he receives that he will fall off, get himself dirty and tear his clothes. He succeeds, but of course also falls off, gets dirty, etc! Physically a very small book, just right for child-sized hands, and a simple story with a real point!
The King Rollo books are published separately in hardback, such as: KING ROLLO'S SPRING Andersen (H); KING ROLLO'S SUMMER Andersen (H); KING ROLLO AND THE LETTER Andersen (H); KING ROLLO AND KING FRANK Andersen (H); KING ROLLO AND THE BALLOON Andersen (H).
There are also editions containing several stories, in hardback and paperback: KING ROLLO'S PLAYROOM AND OTHER STORIES Andersen/Beaver; FURTHER ADVENTURES OF KING ROLLO Beaver (P); KING ROLLO'S LETTER AND OTHER STORIES Andersen/Beaver.
By the same author: THE DAY THE TIDE WENT OUT AND OUT Blackie (P); TUSK TUSK Andersen/Beaver; I HATE MY TEDDY BEAR Andersen/Beaver; TWO ADMIRALS Andersen/Pocket Puffin; WHO'S A CLEVER BABY THEN? Andersen/Beaver; TWO MONSTERS Andersen/Beaver; and others.

MINARIK, ELSE HOLMELUND (Sendak, Maurice)
LITTLE BEAR World's Work/Young Puffin
Short stories about a little bear's domestic adventures, very useful for young readers. Pictures by one of the best-known (and best) illustrators in the business.
In the same series: FATHER BEAR COMES HOME Young Puffin (P); LITTLE BEAR'S FRIEND World's Work (H); LITTLE BEAR STORIES World's Work (H); LITTLE BEAR'S VISIT World's Work/Heinemann.

MURPHY, JILL
* PEACE AT LAST Macmillan (H & P)
Mrs Bear snores so loudly that Mr Bear is kept awake, and each of the other rooms in the house is full of its own noises. In the end he goes back to his own bed, but just as he is falling asleep the alarm clock rings and it is time for a new

day. A lovely picture book, full of life and colour, and very popular with children.
By the same author: FIVE MINUTES PEACE Walker (H & P); WHATEVER NEXT! Macmillan/Picturemac.

OXENBURY, HELEN
THE DANCING CLASS Walker (H & P)
A gentle story about a little girl going to dancing class for the first time. Amusing illustrations, and a delightful series.
In the same series: THE BIRTHDAY PARTY Walker (H & P); EATING OUT Walker (H & P); GRAN AND GRANDPA Walker (H & P); THE DRIVE Walker (H & P) and many others.
By the same author: BILL AND STANLEY A & C Black/Pocket Puffin.

POTTER, BEATRIX
THE TALE OF PETER RABBIT Warne (H)
A book that needs little introduction; a memorable story, and one that successive generations of children have enjoyed. Not an easy read, but ideal for sharing with an individual or small group.
In the same series: THE TALE OF JEMIMA PUDDLE-DUCK Warne (H); THE TALE OF MRS TITTLEMOUSE Warne (H); THE TALE OF BENJAMIN BUNNY Warne (H); and many others. See also THE COMPLETE ADVENTURES OF PETER RABBIT Picture Puffin (P); THE COMPLETE ADVENTURES OF TOM KITTEN AND HIS FRIENDS Picture Puffin (P).

PRATER, JOHN
THE GIFT Bodley Head/Picture Puffin
A magic box is delivered by the postman, and two children playing inside find that it takes off for wild adventures over (and under) the sea. A wordless picture book, and a cleverly told story. Useful for oral retelling.
By the same author: ON FRIDAY SOMETHING FUNNY HAPPENED Picture Puffin; CAN'T CATCH ME! Picture Puffin (P); THE PERFECT DAY Bodley Head/Picture Corgi.

ROGERS, PAUL (Berridge, Celia)
SHEEPCHASE Viking Kestrel/Picture Puffin
A story (in verse) of a lost sheep; if children look at the pictures very carefully they may be able to discover Flossie's hiding places.
By the same author: FORGET-ME-NOT Viking Kestrel/Picture Puffin; TUMBLEDOWN Walker (H).

ROSEN, MICHAEL (Oxenbury, Helen)
WE'RE GOING ON A BEAR HUNT Walker (H)
The traditional rhyme with big print and huge water-colour pictures. Very attractive, and the repetition of the story carries the reader along. Well worth consideration.

SENDAK, MAURICE
* WHERE THE WILD THINGS ARE Bodley Head/Picture Puffin
Max is sent to bed early, but in the night a forest grows in his bedroom, and he sails away to where the wild things are. He tames the monstrous wild things and becomes king, but after a while feels lonely and sails back home to find his supper waiting for him. A classic of modern children's fiction, of the interdependence of words and pictures. A brilliant piece of work, and a sure-fire winner with children! A video version is available from Weston Woods.
By the same author: IN THE NIGHT KITCHEN Bodley Head/Picture Puffin; OUTSIDE OVER THERE Bodley Head/Picture Puffin.

SOWTER, NITA
* MAISIE MIDDLETON Picture Lion (P)
Maisie gets up early, long before Mum and Dad. 'Breakfast please!' she says, and eventually Dad staggers groggily down to the kitchen. But he only succeeds in providing burnt egg, toast and bacon, and even burnt milk, before going back to sleep. So Maisie makes her own delicious breakfast, with a little help from her toy animals. An amusing story with bright and lively pictures.
In the same series: MAISIE MIDDLETON AT THE WEDDING Collins/Picture Lion.

SPIER, PETER
THE FOX WENT OUT ON A CHILLY NIGHT Doubleday (New York) (H)
The traditional song well illustrated. Nicely done.
By the same author: THE BOOK OF JONAH Hodder & Stoughton (H); RAIN Collins (H).

STONES, ROSEMARY AND MANN, ANDREW (Jones, Dan)
* MOTHER GOOSE COMES TO CABLE STREET Picture Puffin (P)
Nursery rhymes set in a modern urban and multicultural context. A clever idea, and many of the rhymes work very well with their new illustrations.

SUTTON, EVE (Dodd, Lynley)
MY CAT LIKES TO HIDE IN BOXES Spindlewood/Picture Puffin
Exuberant pictures of cats from all over the world doing unusual and strange

things, but my very ordinary cat's claim to fame is that he likes to hide in boxes! Very repetitive, but lively enough to keep children interested.

VINCENT, GABRIELLE
BRAVO, ERNEST AND CELESTINE Julia MacRae (H)
A charming story of a bear and a mouse who solve their financial difficulties by improvised busking. All the text is direct speech, so much of the story is carried by the pictures. Thus the book is not quite such an easy read as it appears at first glance.
In the same series: BREAKFAST TIME, ERNEST AND CELESTINE Julia MacRae/Walker; SMILE PLEASE, ERNEST AND CELESTINE Julia MacRae/Picture Lion; and others.

WADDELL, MARTIN (Firth, Barbara)
* CAN'T YOU SLEEP, LITTLE BEAR? Walker (H)
Little Bear is reassuringly shown by Big Bear that the dark is not really so very frightening. A delightful, beautifully illustrated and prize-winning book.
By the same author: ALICE THE ARTIST Little Mammoth (P).

ZIEFERT, HARRIET (Taback, Simms)
* JASON'S BUS RIDE Picture Puffin (P)
Jason is the only passenger on the bus who can get the dog to move out of the way; all it takes is a little kindness. One of a useful series of brightly illustrated books for beginning readers called 'Hello Reading'.
In the same series: HARRY TAKES A BATH Picture Puffin (P); A NEW HOUSE FOR MOLE AND MOUSE Picture Puffin (P); MIKE AND TONY: BEST FRIENDS Picture Puffin (P); NICKY UPSTAIRS AND DOWN Picture Puffin (P); SAY GOODNIGHT Picture Puffin (P).

10
PICTURE BOOKS FOR EXTENDING READING

AHLBERG, ALLAN (Wright, Joe)
* MRS PLUG THE PLUMBER Viking Kestrel/Picture Puffin
On her way home from mending a leak in a lady's bathroom, Mrs Plug sees a rich man being robbed in the street. Out comes her blowlamp, and she fires it right at the robber's bottom, which quickly gets rid of him! The rich man is so grateful that he rewards her with tickets for a voyage round the world. But even on the ship, when there is a storm the captain has to call 'Send for Mrs Plug'! An outstanding series of books: the language is simple, but the stories are ingenious, very amusing, non-sexist, and well-written and illustrated. Highly recommended for all young children.
In the same series: MASTER MONEY THE MILLIONAIRE Viking Kestrel/Puffin; MASTER SALT THE SAILOR'S SON Viking Kestrel/Puffin; MR TICK THE TEACHER Viking Kestrel/Puffin; MISS BRICK THE BUILDER'S BABY Viking Kestrel/Puffin; MRS WOBBLE THE WAITRESS Viking Kestrel/Puffin; MR CREEP THE CROOK Viking Kestrel/Puffin; MRS JOLLY'S JOKE SHOP Viking Kestrel/Puffin; MISS DOSE THE DOCTOR'S DAUGHTER Viking Kestrel/Puffin; and many others.

AHLBERG, JANET AND ALLAN
* THE JOLLY POSTMAN Heinemann (H)
How do the Ahlbergs keep on producing such imaginative and exciting picture books? Luckily they do, and even by their high standards this one is exceptional (and has so far sold over a million copies!). As discussed earlier (pp. 22–4) the book follows a postman delivering letters to all the old nursery rhyme characters, and the very funny letters are included within the book to be taken out and read. A book to appeal to all ages and reading attainments.

* COPS AND ROBBERS Heinemann/Little Mammoth
A hilarious ballad about the forces of law and order in the person of Officer Pugh ('He can run like a hare/And fight like a bear/And he's good at crosswords too'), and six desperate villains who on Christmas Eve are determined to steal all the presents they can lay their hands on. Needless to say, the fiendish plot is foiled by the intrepid policeman! The illustrations are both intricate and very witty.
By the same authors: THE WORM BOOK Picture Lion (P); BYE BYE BABY Heinemann (H).

ALTHEA (Kopper, Lisa)
WHEN UNCLE BOB DIED Dinosaur (P)
One of a series of picture books dealing with real life problems through simple stories, attractively illustrated. These books generally manage to make serious points in the context of an interesting and realistic story. A commendable enterprise.
In the same series: I HAVE ECZEMA Dinosaur (P); I HAVE EPILEPSY Dinosaur (H & P); I CAN'T HEAR LIKE YOU Dinosaur (H); VISITING THE DENTIST Dinosaur (P); and many others.

ANDREW, MARGARET (Lewis, Tracey)
MAC THE MACARONI: THE PENGUIN WHO LIKED TO DANCE Macdonald (H & P)
A lively and amusing story about a macaroni penguin, with large and exuberant pictures.

BRIGGS, RAYMOND
* FATHER CHRISTMAS Hamish Hamilton/Picture Puffin
Father Christmas has every reason to complain – he has to work in terrible weather when almost everyone else is enjoying themselves. And people live in such awkward places: how is he supposed to deliver presents to lighthouses or igloos? Told in strip cartoon format, the grumpy Father Christmas is a delight. Particularly useful for children who need lots of support for their reading, but enormous fun for readers of any age or skill from five year olds to adults.
In the same series: FATHER CHRISTMAS GOES ON HOLIDAY Hamish Hamilton/Picture Puffin; THE COMPLETE FATHER CHRISTMAS Hamish Hamilton/Picture Puffin.
* JIM AND THE BEANSTALK Picture Puffin (P)
When Jim finds a beanstalk growing outside his house he naturally climbs to the top and meets the giant. But the giant is in a bad way: his eyes and his teeth are terrible, and he is almost bald. Jim manages to help him look and feel better, but unfortunately his appetite for fried boys also returns! A clever and novel version of the old story.

BROWN, RUTH

IF AT FIRST YOU DO NOT SEE Andersen/Beaver
A caterpillar thinks sitting on a leaf pretty boring, but gets more than he bargains for when he sets off to find something more exciting to do. A very ingenious book, as the pictures can be viewed upside down as well as right way up.
By the same author: OUR CAT FLOSSIE Andersen (P); CRAZY CHARLIE Andersen/Arrow; OUR PUPPY'S HOLIDAY Andersen/Beaver; THE BIG SNEEZE Andersen/Beaver.

BROWNE, ANTHONY

* GORILLA Julia MacRae/Little Mammoth
Hannah's Dad is far too busy to take much notice of his daughter, let alone take her to the zoo to see her favourite animals. But in the night her toy gorilla grows to full size, and is glad to take Hannah with him to see his brothers and cousins. As she looks at the primates in their cages there is a wonderful line: 'She thought they were beautiful. But sad.' A most engaging story, which can be read in different ways at different levels. The sophisticated illustrations, by an unusual and gifted artist, powerfully contribute to the book's effects. An excellent video version is also available.
A WALK IN THE PARK Hamish Hamilton/Picturemac
Scruffy Mr Smith and posh Mrs Smythe take their respective children and dogs to the park. The children play happily together, but the two adults, of course, solidly ignore each other. Odd, ambiguous and very funny pictures: in the background Tarzan is swinging through the trees, and a man is taking a large pig for a walk! A subtle picture book: both text and pictures have layers of meaning to explore. As with all Anthony Browne's books, very useful for discussion.
By the same author: BEAR HUNT Hamish Hamilton/Hippo; BEAR GOES TO TOWN Hamish Hamilton/Beaver; LOOK WHAT I'VE GOT Julia MacRae/Magnet; PIGGYBOOK Julia MacRae/Little Mammoth; WILLY THE WIMP Julia MacRae/Magnet; WILLY THE CHAMP Julia MacRae (H).

BURNINGHAM, JOHN

* COME AWAY FROM THE WATER, SHIRLEY Cape/Picture Lion
'Of course it's far too cold for swimming, Shirley,' say Mum and Dad as they settle down in their deck chairs for a rather boring day on the beach. But Shirley does not hear: she is off to the pirate ship, walking the plank, escaping with a map showing hidden treasure, and digging up a huge box of gold and jewels. A brilliantly imaginative book, outstanding in every way (see also pp. 20–22).
In the same series: TIME TO GET OUT OF THE BATH, SHIRLEY Cape/Picture Lion.

* GRANPA Cape/Picture Puffin
A lovely book about the relationship between a little girl and her grandfather. Subtly and sensitively done; the final sad picture seems completely appropriate.

COLE, BABETTE
* PRINCESS SMARTYPANTS Hamish Hamilton/Picture Lion
Princess Smartypants does not want to marry any boring old prince; she wants to live with her pets and do just as she pleases. So she sets very difficult tasks for various princes to complete in order to win her hand. Unfortunately, Prince Swashbuckle accomplishes them all with ease, but Princess Smartypants still has a final trick up her sleeve! A good feminist story, with absurdly appropriate illustrations.
By the same author: THE TROUBLE WITH DAD Heinemann/Picture Lion; THE TROUBLE WITH MUM Picture Lion (P); THE TROUBLE WITH GRAN Heinemann/Picture Lion; THE TROUBLE WITH GRANDAD Heinemann/Little Mammoth; THREE CHEERS FOR ERROL Heinemann/Mammoth.

CUTLER, IVOR (Oxenbury, Helen)
MEAL ONE Heinemann/Picture Lion
Helbert thinks that growing a huge plum tree in his bedroom is a great idea, until he discovers that the roots of the tree have reached down into the kitchen and are swallowing his breakfast. Luckily Mum is a resourceful lady who finds a novel way of solving the problem. A bizarre but very clever story, skilfully illustrated.
By the same author: THE ANIMAL HOUSE Heinemann/Little Mammoth

DALY, NIKI
NOT SO FAST SONGOLOLO Gollancz/Picture Puffin
An old African lady and her grandson go shopping in the big city; not so fast, she calls, as he rushes ahead. She buys him a pair of new red 'tackies' at the shoe shop before they have to make their way home again. Set in South Africa; much is implied about that country.
By the same author: JOSEPH'S OTHER RED SOCK Picture Lion (P); LEO'S CHRISTMAS SURPRISE Picture Lion (P).

DUPASQUIER, PHILIPPE
JACK AT SEA Andersen/Picture Puffin
When McCloud is press-ganged into the Navy young Jack decides to follow. They both find that life at sea is terribly hard, and when the enemy is sighted and battle begins it is very dangerous too. Realistic and quite exciting adventures in

which the pictures carry most of the story line.
By the same author: DEAR DADDY ... Andersen/Picture Puffin; OUR
HOUSE ON THE HILL Andersen/Picture Puffin; ROBERT THE GREAT
Walker (P).

GAGE, WILSON (Hefner, Marylin)
MRS GADDY AND THE GHOST Hippo (P)
Mrs Gaddy is determined to get rid of the ghost which haunts her house, but it
resists all her efforts. Eventually she realizes that the ghost is part of the house,
and if it did go she would miss it! One of a popular series.
In the same series: MRS GADDY AND THE FAST GROWING VINE
Bodley Head (H); THE CROW AND MRS GADDY Hippo (P).

GRAHAM, BOB
PEARL'S PLACE Picture Lion (P)
Living in a tall block of flats is not much fun for Arthur — there is nowhere to
play and no space to keep a pet. But Pearl's place is a wonderful contrast: a pond
in the garden, cats, dogs, budgies and lots to do. Pearl even says that Arthur and
his Mum can come and stay! A lively picture book, plenty of action.
By the same author: FIRST THERE WAS FRANCES Picture Lion (P); THE
WILD Picture Lion (P); PETE AND ROWLAND Picture Lion (P).

HENDERSON, KATHY
* FIFTEEN WAYS TO GO TO BED Frances Lincoln (P)
Lively illustrated story-poems about bedtime: reasons for staying up; monsters
that may strike; being ill in bed; babysitters; and my favourite (from bitter
experience), a poem about children who are raucously loud on a car journey and
then fall asleep two minutes from home.
In the same series: FIFTEEN WAYS TO GET DRESSED Windward (H).
By the same author: THE BABYSITTER Deutsch (H).

HERSOM, KATHLEEN (Daly, Niki)
MAYBE IT'S A TIGER Picturemac (P)
A group of children play at zoos, using their toy pets as animals. Somehow they
fail to notice what is going on in the street behind them, where some really fierce
creatures are frightening the life out of all the passers-by! A useful story, where
alternative meanings are carried by the pictures.

HOBAN, RUSSELL (Hoban, Lilian)
BEST FRIENDS FOR FRANCES Hippo (P)
Even though Albert will not let her join in with his games, Frances decides that it

is best to include him in the outing, since he can play a useful part. Quite a complex text, but the pictures provide just enough support to carry the reader along.

In the same series: A BIRTHDAY FOR FRANCES Hippo (P); BREAD AND JAM FOR FRANCES Picture Puffin (P).

HOLLICK, HELEN (Cope, Jane)
COME AND TELL ME Dinosaur (P)
How children can cope with strangers' requests (by asking Mum first) in the context of a simple story.

HUGHES, SHIRLEY
* ALFIE GETS IN FIRST Bodley Head/Picture Lion
Alfie locks himself in the house, leaving Mum outside on the doorstep. All the neighbours gather to proffer advice and help, and the window cleaner even climbs his ladder to try to get in the bathroom window. Meanwhile, clever Alfie has worked out a way of opening the door himself, and proudly does so. Language is a bit difficult for children to read by themselves, but a useful book to read with a group.

In the same series: ALFIE'S FEET Bodley Head/Picture Lion; ALFIE GIVES A HAND Bodley Head/Picture Lion; AN EVENING AT ALFIE'S Bodley Head/Picture Lion.
By the same author: DOGGER Bodley Head/Picture Lion; HELPERS Bodley Head/Picture Lion; UP AND UP Bodley Head/Picture Lion.

JANOSCH
LITTLE TIGER, GET WELL SOON! Andersen/Hippo
All the animals gather round to help Little Tiger when he falls ill. Indeed, Little Tiger seems to be having such a good time that at the end of the book his friend Little Bear decides that next time it is his turn to be ill. A quirky little story; lots of humorous detail in the illustrations.

In the same series: A LETTER FOR TIGER Andersen (H).
By the same author: THE LITTLE HARE BOOK Pocket Puffin (P); THE TRIP TO PANAMA Andersen/Picturemac.

JONAS, ANN
THE TREK Julia MacRae (H)
A little girl negotiates her way to school through what at first glance appears to be an ordinary suburb. But look closer and you can see an amazing variety of animals like elephants, tigers and hippos! How many different ones can be found?

By the same author: WHERE CAN IT BE? Julia MacRae (H); HOLES AND PEEKS Walker (P); NOW WE CAN GO Julia MacRae/Walker.

KERR, JUDITH
* MOG AND THE BABY Collins/Picture Lion
'Will Mog be all right with the baby?' says Nicky. 'Oh yes,' says Mrs Thomas, 'Mog loves babies.' The expression on poor Mog's face suggests otherwise, especially when the baby eats her fish! But heroic Mog dashes to the rescue when the baby gets out into the road and is about to be run over. A popular book with young children.
In the same series: MOG THE FORGETFUL CAT Collins/Picture Lion; MOG'S CHRISTMAS Collins/Picture Lion; MOG IN THE DARK Collins/Picture Lion; and others.
By the same author: THE TIGER WHO CAME TO TEA Collins/Picture Lion.

LAMONT, PRISCILLA
THE TROUBLESOME PIG Hamish Hamilton/Piccolo
The well-known nursery story of the pig who will not jump over the stile. Nor will the water quench the fire, or the fire burn the stick, or the stick beat the dog, or the dog bite the pig (etcetera, etcetera) until the ginger cat comes along. A repetitive but enjoyable story.

LEWIS, ROB
THE GREAT GRANNY ROBBERY Macdonald (H & P)
Len the Laugher kidnaps grannies and takes them to secret factories where they have to knit woolly jumpers and socks all day long to make money. But when all the meanest and toughest grannies are mobilized, Len and his gang are no match for them. Absurd, but great fun.
By the same author: HELLO MR SCARECROW Macdonald (H & P); COME BACK HERCULES Macdonald (H & P).

MAHY, MARGARET (Williams, Jenny)
* A LION IN THE MEADOW Dent/Picture Puffin
A little boy is frightened by a lion in the meadow, so his mother gives him a matchbox which she says has a dragon inside it, to scare the lion away. But the little boy and the lion become friends, and the dragon goes to sleep quietly. A lovely story, something of a modern classic, and beautifully illustrated.
By the same author: THE MAN WHOSE MOTHER WAS A PIRATE Dent/Picture Puffin; THE WITCH IN THE CHERRY TREE Dent/Picture Puffin; 17 KINGS AND 42 ELEPHANTS Dent/Picture Lion.

MOORE, CLEMENT (Ives, Penny)
THE NIGHT BEFORE CHRISTMAS Orchard (H)
There are many versions of this famous poem about St Nicholas and his reindeer; this one has particularly ingenious illustrations.

MURPHY, JILL
* ON THE WAY HOME Macmillan/Picturemac
As Claire is on her way home she tells the friends she meets somewhat different stories of how she hurt her knee. Was it the big bad wolf, or an alien from a space ship, or a crocodile that caused the problem? Or a snake, or a dragon, or a gorilla, perhaps? Or a giant or a ghost or a witch? It is only when Claire reaches home and Mum that the real story emerges! A justly popular book; appropriately repetitive and very well illustrated.

PEPPE, RODNEY
* THE KETTLESHIP PIRATES Viking Kestrel/Picture Puffin
Lots of exciting adventures as Pip and the kettleship pirates search for buried treasure, and try to overcome the wicked Captain Rat. An energetic picture book, inspired by 'Treasure Island'. Excellent for early readers, and very popular with children.
By the same author: THE MICE AND THE FLYING BASKET Viking Kestrel/Picture Puffin; THE MICE AND THE CLOCKWORK BUS Viking Kestrel/Picture Puffin; THE MICE WHO LIVED IN A SHOE Viking Kestrel/Picture Puffin.

PIENKOWSKI, JAN
* CHRISTMAS Heinemann/Picture Puffin
The glorious words of the Christmas story from the authorized version of the Bible, accompanied by inspired and almost magical illustrations. The best book about Christmas for children, in my opinion, and justifiably admired by adults too.
* HAUNTED HOUSE Heinemann (H)
A skeleton in the cupboard, a crocodile in the bath and something very nasty indeed in the attic! Fascinating, scary and very cleverly put together. One of the best pop up books around.
By the same author: DINNER TIME Orchard (H); ROBOT Heinemann (H); FANCY THAT! Orchard (H).

PIRANI, FELIX (Roche, Christine)
ABIGAIL AT THE BEACH Collins/Picture Lion

Abigail's huge sandcastle is threatened by an assortment of boys, girls, dogs, bikes and even Martians! Fortunately, however, she scares them off by referring to her Dad, who is in the Mafia (or the Marines, or the Secret Service). All about the power of children's imagination, and very well done.

In the same series: ABIGAIL GOES VISITING Collins (H).

QUACKENBUSH, ROBERT

HENRY'S AWFUL MISTAKE Collins (H & P)

Henry the duck finds an ant in his kitchen while he is cooking dinner. His desperate attempts to catch the ant result in the destruction of his house. The next time Henry sees an ant in his kitchen he decides to look the other way! One of a useful series of brightly illustrated and high interest picture books with fairly simple texts called 'Help Your Child'.

In the same series: **Davies, Gillian** WHY WORMS? Collins (H & P); **Rowe, Amy and Philip** ERNEST THE FIERCE MOUSE Collins (H & P); **Wilmer, Diane** THE PLAYGROUND Collins (H & P); **Wilmer, Diane** GALLOP OFF AND GO! Collins (H & P); **Wilmer, Diane** ZAP ZERO THE DESPATCH RIDER Collins (H & P); **Cresswell, Helen** THE WEATHER CAT Collins (H & P); and many others.

RAYNER, MARY

CROCODARLING Collins/Picture Lion

Sam is not too keen on school, and in particular he cannot cope with the bullying Henry. But Sam's crocodarling helps him sort everything out! A nice story about dealing with the big world of school.

By the same author: GARTH PIG AND THE ICE CREAM LADY Macmillan/Picturemac.

RICHARDSON, JEAN (Englander, Alice)

TALL INSIDE Picture Puffin (P)

Jo worries about being rather small for her age. But then she meets Lofty, a street clown who seems to be the tallest person in the world. It does not matter what size you are on the outside, he says, as long as you feel tall inside. A good story, and not only for children who are on the small side!

By the same author: CLARA'S DANCING FEET Methuen/Picture Puffin; A DOG FOR BEN Methuen/Picture Puffin.

ROSE, GERALD

THE BAG OF WIND Bodley Head/Magnet

A greedy man agrees to swop all his possessions (and even his wife) for a bag which the sailor says contains nothing but wind, although his parrot keeps on

screeching 'Diamonds and rubies!' When the bag is finally opened, the wind blows the greedy man far away, never to be seen again. A satisfying (and highly moral!) modern folk tale.
By the same author: THE BIRD GARDEN Magnet (P); TROUBLE IN THE ARK Bodley Head/Magnet; WOLF! WOLF! Methuen (H); THE LION AND THE MOUSE Methuen (H); THE HARE AND THE TORTOISE Methuen (H); THE RAVEN AND THE FOX Methuen (H).

ROSS, TONY
TOWSER AND THE WATER RATS Andersen (H)
Towser enjoys lazing about in his holiday house by the river. But when his peace and quiet is disturbed by villainous water rats he takes great pleasure in profiting from their greed. Clever and amusing story.
In the same series: TOWSER AND THE HAUNTED HOUSE Andersen (H); TOWSER AND THE TERRIBLE THING Andersen/Picture Lion; TOWSER AND SADIE'S BIRTHDAY Andersen/Picture Lion.
THE THREE PIGS Andersen (H)
A modern version of the old story with zany illustrations.
By the same author: HANSEL AND GRETEL Andersen (H); PUSS IN BOOTS Pocket Puffin (P); THE BOY WHO CRIED WOLF Andersen/ Beaver; JACK THE GIANTKILLER Andersen (H); I'M COMING TO GET YOU! Andersen/Picture Puffin; I WANT MY POTTY! Andersen/Picture Lion; SOOPER DOOPER JEZEBEL Andersen/Picture Lion.

RYAN, JOHN
CAPTAIN PUGWASH AND THE MIDNIGHT FEAST Young Puffin (P)
When Pugwash's crew decide to hold a midnight feast they are rudely interrupted by Cut-throat Jake and his villainous crew! As ludicrous as all the other Pugwash stories, but great fun.
In the same series: CAPTAIN PUGWASH Bodley Head/Picture Puffin; PUGWASH IN THE PACIFIC Picture Puffin (P); and others.

SEFTON, CATHERINE (Ursell, Martin)
THE GHOST-SHIP Hamish Hamilton (H)
A ghost-ship suddenly appears in the back garden, complete with pirates, skull and crossbones and all. But when the pirates make a terrible mess of things, Bill finds it hard to convince Dad that he was not responsible! A simple but imaginative story.

SMITH, PETER (Graham, Bob)
JENNY'S BABY BROTHER Picture Lion (P)

Jenny's little brother is no fun to play with at all; all he does is lie around and gurgle. But then one day he gets some custard in his spoon, takes aim and flicks it straight into Jenny's eye; and later he trips her up, quite deliberately. Mum and Dad are horrified, but Jenny is secretly delighted! A perceptive book about family relationships.

STEVENSON, JAMES
THE NIGHT AFTER CHRISTMAS Picture Lion (P)
A sad little story of a teddy and a rag doll replaced by a space gun and a Cindy doll respectively, and thrown out into the dustbin. They both find it hard to get used to being unwanted, in spite of help from Chauncey, a stray mongrel. However, in the end they find that there are still children who value them.
By the same author: WORSE THAN WILLY Picture Piper (P); THERE'S NOTHING TO DO! Gollancz/Piccolo.

TROUGHTON, JOANNA
WHAT MADE TIDDALIK LAUGH Blackie (H)
Tiddalik the giant frog drinks so much water that the land becomes parched and dry. The other animals decide that, if they make him laugh, all the water inside him will come spilling out again. They try various strategies unsuccessfully, until the platypus appears, a sight so peculiar that even Tiddalik cannot keep a straight face! An aboriginal folk tale, attractively retold and illustrated.
In the same series: HOW THE RABBIT STOLE THE FIRE Blackie (H); HOW THE BIRDS CHANGED THEIR FEATHERS Blackie (H); TORTOISE'S DREAM Blackie (H); HOW NIGHT CAME: A FOLK TALE FROM THE AMAZON Blackie (H); THE WIZARD PUNCHKIN: A FOLK TALE FROM INDIA Blackie (H).

WADDELL, MARTIN (Dupasquier, Philippe)
* GOING WEST Andersen/Picture Puffin
A pioneer family heads west across America to find a new home. On the way they meet and overcome many dangers: storms, disease and hostile Indians. Most of the story is carried by the superb panoramic pictures which contrast most effectively with the deliberately minimal text. Very effective; good value.
By the same author: THE GREAT GREEN MOUSE DISASTER Walker (H & P); THE BUDGIE SAID GRRRR! Methuen (H); THE TOUGH PRINCESS Walker (H & P).

WILLIS, JEANNE (Chamberlain, Margaret)
* THE TALE OF FEARSOME FRITZ Andersen/Beaver
Fritz dresses up as a gorilla for a visit to the zoo. The keeper checks that the real

gorilla is still in his cage, but gets in a muddle and leaves the door open. Realizing his error, the keeper catches the gorilla (i.e. Fritz) and locks him in the cage, while Mum takes the real gorilla home for tea. Very funny doggerel verse with lively illustrations.

By the same author: THE TALE OF MUCKY MABEL Andersen/Beaver; THE TALE OF GEORGIE GRUB Andersen/Beaver.

ZOLOTOW, CHARLOTTE (Sendak, Maurice)
MR RABBIT AND THE LOVELY PRESENT Bodley Head/Picture Puffin
With the help of rabbit, a little girl constructs a lovely present of a basket of fruit for her mother. A repetitive but imaginative storyline, and illustrations by a master of his art.

11
PICTURE BOOKS FOR INDEPENDENT READING

AARDEMA, VERNA (Chess, Victoria)
PRINCESS GORILLA AND A NEW KIND OF WATER Bodley Head/Piper
King Gorilla decrees that whoever can drink a barrel of liquid that he has found
by the roadside may marry his daughter. Many animals try, but they all fail since
the barrel is full of most unpleasant vinegar, and the princess is left to marry the
handsome young gorilla that she wanted from the beginning. An interesting
retelling of a traditional African folk tale.
By the same author: BRINGING THE RAIN TO KAPITI PLAIN Picturemac
(P); OH KOJO! HOW COULD YOU? Picturemac (P); BIMWILI AND THE
ZIMWI: A TALE FROM ZANZIBAR Picturemac (P); RABBIT MAKES A
MONKEY OUT OF LION Bodley Head (H).

ARDIZZONE, EDWARD
TIM'S LAST VOYAGE Picturemac (P)
Tim and Ginger sign on as temporary deckhands on the SS *Arabella*. They get
more adventures than they bargained for when a huge storm blows up. Written
and illustrated by one of the acknowledged masters of the picture book form.
Seems a bit old-fashioned in style now, but still a good story.
In the same series: LITTLE TIM AND THE BRAVE SEA CAPTAIN Viking
Kestrel/Picture Puffin; TIM IN DANGER Oxford University Press (P); TIM
TO THE RESCUE Oxford University Press/Picture Puffin; TIM'S FRIEND
TOWSER Oxford University Press (P); and others.

ARMITAGE, RONDA AND DAVID
ICE CREAMS FOR ROSIE Deutsch (H)
When the ice cream runs out at Rosie's shop a parachute drop is needed to avert
a crisis. But the bag bursts, and ice creams are scattered all over the island. Rosie

has a difficult time rescuing all her delicious ice creams before they melt! A lively and colourful story.

By the same authors: DON'T FORGET MATILDA Deutsch (H); THE LIGHTHOUSE KEEPER'S LUNCH Deutsch/Picture Puffin; THE LIGHTHOUSE KEEPER'S CATASTROPHE Deutsch/Picture Puffin; THE LIGHTHOUSE KEEPER'S RESCUE Deutsch (H); GRANDMA GOES SHOPPING Deutsch/Picture Puffin.

BEISNER, MONIKA
SECRET SPELLS AND CURIOUS CHARMS Cape (H)
Surrealistic pictures accompanying charms and spells for every occasion. If you wish for revenge, for love, for fortune, then here are the appropriate incantations! Could form the basis of an interesting exploration of language and the power of words.

BIRD, MALCOLM
* THE WITCH'S HANDBOOK Beaver (P)
A marvellous book, full of inventive ideas (most of which really work) and imaginative illustrations. Spells, superstitions, recipes, crafts, cookery, gardening, fortune-telling, and even a section on careers! Very funny, and guaranteed to keep children entertained.

BIRO, VAL
GUMDROP: THE ADVENTURES OF A VINTAGE CAR Hodder & Stoughton (H)
Lots of technical detail in this story of Bill McArran's rescue and rebuilding of an old and almost disintegrated Austin Clifton Twelve Four. Thus not an easy read, but ideal for children fascinated by talk of carburettors and ammeters and so on. One of a large and enduring series.

In the same series: GUMDROP FINDS A GHOST Hodder & Stoughton/ Picture Puffin; GUMDROP GETS HIS WINGS Picture Puffin (P); GUMDROP AND THE MONSTER Picture Puffin (P); GUMDROP ON THE MOVE Hodder & Stoughton (H); GUMDROP AT SEA Hodder & Stoughton (H); GUMDROP'S MAGIC JOURNEY Hodder & Stoughton (H); GUMDROP ON THE RALLY Hodder & Stoughton/Picture Knight; and many others.
By the same author: DRANGO DRAGON Ladybird (H).

BLUME, JUDY (Trivas, Irene)
* THE PAIN AND THE GREAT ONE Heinemann/Piper
A wonderfully witty book about the tribulations of being brother and sister.

Each thinks the other has all the treats, gets away with terrible behaviour, and is Mum and Dad's favourite. And each discovers that it is even less fun to play alone!

BRIGGS, RAYMOND
FUNGUS THE BOGEYMAN Hamish Hamilton (H & P)
All the most disgusting and revolting aspects of human behaviour are personified in the character and adventures of Fungus. A book that was recently (and accurately) summarized as 'an anthology of bad taste'! Popular with older children, but to a sensitive adult's eyes absolutely nauseating at first. The book is more subtle than it seems though; worth looking at closely. Raymond Briggs' cartoon strip picture books are really the only ones in the same class as Goscinny and Uderzo's Asterix series and the Tintin books by Hergé. Excellent for older readers.
By the same author: GENTLEMAN JIM Hamish Hamilton (H & P); UNLUCKY WALLY Hamish Hamilton (H); WHEN THE WIND BLOWS Penguin (P).

CARTWRIGHT, ANN (Cartwright, Reg)
* NORAH'S ARK Hutchinson/Picture Puffin
Resourceful Norah manages to rescue all her animals in spite of the flood. A clever modern version of the familiar story, very appropriately illustrated.
By the same author: THE PROUD AND FEARLESS LION Hutchinson/Beaver.

COLE, BABETTE
* NUNGU AND THE CROCODILE (out of print)
A very complicated story of the absurd love affair between Kangwa the crocodile and Poffo the ostrich. All ends happily, but not before several equally unlikely characters have joined in! A very funny story, matched by wonderfully ridiculous illustrations. Very popular with children.
In the same series: NUNGU AND THE ELEPHANT Collins (H).
By the same author: BEWARE OF THE VET Hamish Hamilton/Little Mammoth.

CRABTREE, JUDITH
THE SPARROW'S STORY AT THE KING'S COMMAND Oxford University Press (H)
A resourceful sparrow fulfils the storyteller's dying wish by taking his last story to the king; but the tale of his own adventures en route is even more dramatic. An unusual story, with a moral point.

DAHL, ROALD (Blake, Quentin)
* THE ENORMOUS CROCODILE Cape/Picture Puffin
'I'm off to find a yummy child for lunch. Keep listening and you'll hear the bones go crunch!' The inimitable Dahl tells the story of the crocodile's attempts to find a child or two to eat by the use of 'clever tricks' like lying across a log pretending to be a see-saw. Luckily all his fiendish schemes are foiled, but only just! Exuberant pictures, and a very popular book.
* REVOLTING RHYMES Cape/Picture Puffin
Six of the old fairy stories ('Jack and the Beanstalk', 'Cinderella', etc.) retold in verse, and in each case given a new and startling twist. For example, Cinderella is portrayed as a juvenile delinquent; and if the wolf had known what kind of a girl Little Red Riding Hood was he would have avoided her at all costs! A brilliant piece of work, and very funny indeed, although some teachers might feel that it is a little earthy in parts!
By the same author: DIRTY BEASTS Cape/Picture Puffin; THE GIRAFFE AND THE PELLY AND ME Cape/Picture Puffin.

DE GEREZ, TONI (Cooney, Barbara)
LOUHI, WITCH OF THE NORTH FARM Julia MacRae/Picture Puffin
Louhi the witch feels mischievous, and so steals the sun and the moon. Only the combined skills of the god-like Vainomoinen and the blacksmith Seppo can force her to replace them. An imaginative retelling of a Finnish story, dramatically illustrated. A useful introduction to European folk tales.

FOREMAN, MICHAEL
* WAR AND PEAS Picture Puffin (P)
The Fat King not only refuses to help his starving neighbours in King Lion's country, but also chases them away with his soldiers. In the end, though, as the Fat King finds, war can turn into peas! A brilliant moral fable about the relationship between rich and poor countries, with huge pictures of food providing the landscape for the action. Highly recommended: plenty of scope for discussion and activities here.
By the same author: DINOSAURS AND ALL THAT RUBBISH Picture Puffin (P); PANDA'S PUZZLE AND HIS VOYAGE OF DISCOVERY Hamish Hamilton/Pocket Puffin; THE ANGEL AND THE WILD ANIMAL Andersen/Beaver; LAND OF DREAMS Andersen (H).

FRASCINO, EDWARD
MY COUSIN THE KING Dent (H)
The farmer's cat lets a circus lion out of his cage, thinking he is in the same royal family as the king of beasts. The lion, however, is more interested in viewing the

farmyard animals as dinner than as loyal subjects! A funny parable, wittily illustrated.

FURCHGOTT, TERRY AND DAWSON, LINDA (Furchgott, Terry)
PHOEBE AND THE HOT WATER BOTTLES Deutsch (H)
Phoebe's Dad is a bit absent minded, and keeps giving her presents of hot water bottles for Christmas and birthdays. Phoebe thinks hot water bottles are all very well, but they are not very affectionate! And Dad thinks she is too young to look after the puppy that she really wants. But when the house catches fire, brave Phoebe finds the hot water bottles very useful, and grateful Dad at last relents. An unusual and entertaining story.

GANLY, HELEN
* JYOTI'S JOURNEY Deutsch (H)
Little Jyoti travels from the exuberant colour and life of India to grey and cold England. What kind of life will she find there? Wonderful collage pictures, and useful for discussion of human migration.

GERRARD, ROY
SIR CEDRIC RIDES AGAIN Gollancz (H)
Weedy Hubert saves Sir Cedric's lively daughter Edwina from a fate worse than death when she is captured by Abdul the Heavy. Hilarious doggerel verse, and very funny pictures too.
In the same series: SIR CEDRIC Gollancz (H & P).

GOSCINNY, RENE (Uderzo, M.)
* ASTERIX IN BRITAIN Hodder & Stoughton (H & P)
One of many cartoon stories about Asterix the Gaul and his friends; in this one Asterix takes on the supposed might of the Roman army in Britain. The action is unceasing and very lively, and there is lots of humour, especially when mocking stereotypes of British characteristics (fighting stops for tea in mid-afternoon). Excellent for older children who find reading difficult since the pictures carry much of the story along; highly recommended.
In the same series: ASTERIX THE GAUL Hodder & Stoughton (H & P); ASTERIX THE LEGIONARY Hodder & Stoughton (H & P); ASTERIX AND THE ROMAN AGENT Hodder & Stoughton (H & P); ASTERIX AND THE GOTHS Hodder & Stoughton (H & P); and many others.

HAWKINS, COLIN AND JACQUI
SPOOKS Granada/Picture Lion
A mock handbook: over-the-top pictures and lots of terrible jokes which will

appeal to all nine year olds. A boisterous series, and often very funny. In the same series: VAMPIRES Picture Lion (P); WITCHES Granada/Picture Lion; PIRATES Collins/Picture Lion. A compendium of WITCHES, VAMPIRES and SPOOKS is also available, titled SHRIEK, Granada (H).

HERGÉ
* THE ADVENTURES OF TINTIN: PRISONERS OF THE SUN Methuen (H & P)
Resourceful Tintin in an exciting adventure set in Peru. Like the Asterix stories, the Tintin books are excellent for older primary school children: fast and direct adventures, with plenty of action, written in cartoon strip format. The pictures carry much of the story, but the language is also at times quite complex ('You miserable iconoclast!'). Very popular and enjoyable.
In the same series: TINTIN IN AMERICA Methuen (H & P); TINTIN AND THE PICAROS Methuen (H & P); TINTIN IN TIBET Methuen (H & P); and many others.

HOBAN, RUSSELL (Blake, Quentin)
* THE RAIN DOOR Gollancz/Picturemac
On a fiercely hot summer's day Harry somehow follows a rag-and-bone man through the rain door into a vast desert, where the rain is collected. There he meets a lion, a dinosaur that hoots 'Gahooga!' and a horse called Lightning, but his adventures are only just beginning! A lively and inventive story, much enhanced by Quentin Blake's witty and imaginative illustrations.
By the same author: HOW TOM BEAT CAPTAIN NAJORK AND HIS HIRED SPORTSMEN Cape/Young Piper; THE DANCING TIGERS Cape (H); THEY CAME FROM AARGH! Walker (P); THE TWENTY ELEPHANT RESTAURANT Cape/Pocket Puffin; ACE DRAGON LIMITED Cape/Magnet.

HOFFMAN, MARY (Jaques, Faith)
THE RETURN OF THE ANTELOPE Heinemann/Picture Puffin
Three engaging but tiny people from Gulliver's Lilliput are shipwrecked in our enormous world. Luckily they meet Philippa and Gerald, friendly and helpful children, who do their best to assist. Based on a recent television series.
By the same author: MY GRANDMA HAS BLACK HAIR Methuen (H).

KEEPING, CHARLES AND CROSSLEY-HOLLAND, KEVIN
* BEOWULF Oxford University Press (B & W) (P)
The bloodthirsty old story well retold, with Charles Keeping's magnificent black and white pictures. Beowulf's monstrous opponents are wonderfully drawn;

to my amateur eye genuine works of art. As discussed in Chapter 2, Keeping has produced similarly superb illustrations for Alfred Noyes' THE HIGHWAYMAN Oxford University Press (H), and for Alfred, Lord Tennyson's THE LADY OF SHALOTT Oxford University Press (H & P). By the same author (Charles Keeping): SAMMY STREETSINGER Oxford University Press (H).

KINMONTH, PATRICK (Cartwright, Reg)
MR POTTER'S PIGEON Pocket Puffin (P)
Mr Potter's pigeon gets lost, and only returns just in time for the race. But its earlier explorations prove useful in the foggy conditions, and Mr Potter's pigeon wins first prize.

LEWIS, NAOMI (Castle, Barry)
CRY WOLF AND OTHER AESOP FABLES Methuen (H)
The famous moral stories, with distinctive illustrations.

LINDGREN, ASTRID (Wikland, Ilon)
THE GHOST OF SKINNY JACK Methuen (H)
When Grandma tells the story of how Skinny Jack's ghost haunted the village where she was born, the children find it exciting but rather scary. But then to have to walk home through a dark wood as night falls is absolutely terrifying! A good story within a story; and the pictures add much to the threatening atmosphere.
By the same author: LOTTA Methuen (H); LOTTA'S BIKE Methuen (H); LOTTA'S CHRISTMAS SURPRISE Magnet (P); and others.

LONGFELLOW, HENRY WADSWORTH (Le Cain, Errol)
* HIAWATHA'S CHILDHOOD Faber/Picture Puffin
The beginning of Longfellow's famous poem, in which Hiawatha grows up. He learns the stories and legends of his people, and how to make friends with all the wild animals. Wonderful illustrations that seem to glow with warmth and colour.

MAHY, MARGARET (Craig, Helen)
JAM Dent/Magnet
When Mr Castle decides to make plum jam, he does it thoroughly. In fact, there is so much that the children get absolutely fed up with having to eat it all. Eventually the very last pot is eaten, but unfortunately a whole year has gone by and the plums on the tree are ripe once again! A funny and realistic story.

McCRUM, ROBERT (Foreman, Michael)
THE BRONTOSAURUS BIRTHDAY CAKE Hamish Hamilton/Magnet
Bobby is so keen on dinosaurs that Mum makes a brontosaurus birthday cake.
But when it comes alive and starts growing bigger and bigger, certain problems
of a dinosaur as a pet become apparent. Nice book for children interested in the
subject, and beautifully illustrated, but not the easiest of texts.
In the same series: BRONTOSAURUS SUPERSTAR! Magnet (P); THE
DREAM BOAT BRONTOSAURUS Hamish Hamilton (H).

McNAUGHTON, COLIN
FOOTBALL CRAZY Heinemann/Little Mammoth
Bruno the bear is only picked as substitute for Tex's Tygers, but when he comes
on to play he really shows them what he can do, until he gives away a penalty!
Witty pictures that capture the excitement of the game.
By the same author: CRAZY BEAR Heinemann (H); FAT PIG Black/Pocket
Puffin; KING NONN THE WISER Heinemann/Pocket Puffin; THE RAT
RACE Walker (P); SANTA CLAUS IS SUPERMAN Walker (P); THE
GREAT ZOO ESCAPE Heinemann/Little Mammoth.

OAKLEY, GRAHAM
* THE CHURCH MICE ADRIFT Macmillan/Picturemac
Sampson the cat feels that his reputation rests on evicting the rats who have
taken over the mice's vestry home. He manages it in the end, but not without a
struggle. Highly anthropomorphic animals, inventive text with a delightful dry
humour (although not an easy read), very subtle and clever satire. The faces of
both cat and mice are so expressive that they complement the storyline
perfectly.
In the same series: THE CHURCH MOUSE Macmillan/Picturemac; THE
CHURCH MICE AT BAY Picturemac (P); THE CHURCH MICE AT
CHRISTMAS Macmillan/Picturemac; THE CHURCH MICE IN ACTION
Macmillan (H); THE CHURCH MICE SPREAD THEIR WINGS Macmillan/
Picturemac; and others. An omnibus THE CHURCH MICE CHRONICLES
Macmillan (H) is also available.

ORAM, HIAWYN (Kitamura, Satoshi)
NED AND THE JOYBALOO Andersen/Beaver
The Joybaloo happily comes out to play with Ned on Friday nights. But then
Ned insists that the strange creature should play every night in spite of its
protests that it needs to sleep. Gradually it fades away, until there is no Joybaloo
left at all, and Ned has to try to find ways of being joyful all by himself.
By the same author: ANGRY ARTHUR Andersen/Picture Puffin; JUST LIKE
US Orchard (H); IN THE ATTIC Andersen/Beaver.

PIERS, HELEN (Foreman, Michael)
* LONG NECK AND THUNDERFOOT Viking Kestrel/Picture Puffin
When two peaceful dinosaurs meet, they each believe the other is a fierce and monstrous creature. Not until they convince themselves that they have nothing to fear can they get together and organize a party for all the animals. Brilliant pictures by Michael Foreman, one of the best illustrators around.

STEINER, JORG (Muller, Jorg)
THE BEAR WHO WANTED TO STAY A BEAR Andersen (H)
A big brown bear finds his familiar habitat has disappeared to be replaced by a huge modern factory. In spite of his protestations that he is a bear, he is accused of being just a dirty, lazy worker who needs a shave. A sad but important story of man's inhumanity to animals.

STORR, CATHERINE (Dzierzek, Anna)
* ANDROCLES AND THE LION Methuen (P)
Literate retelling of the famous story with colourful illustrations. This book is one of a series of retold versions of classic stories collectively titled 'Great Tales from Long Ago'. They vary in quality, but are generally very useful. **Berrill, Margaret** THE CANTERBURY TALES: CHANTICLEER Methuen (P); **Berrill, Margaret** SIR GAWAIN AND THE GREEN KNIGHT Methuen (P); **Berrill, Margaret** BEOWULF AND THE MONSTERS Methuen (P); **Hunter, Mollie** FLORA MACDONALD AND BONNIE PRINCE CHARLIE Methuen (P); **Lawrence, Ann** MERLIN THE WIZARD Methuen (P); **Storr, Catherine** THE PIED PIPER OF HAMELIN Methuen (P); **Storr, Catherine** RICHARD THE LIONHEART Methuen (P); **Trotman, Felicity** WILLIAM TELL Methuen (P); **Trotman, Felicity** THE TRAVELS OF MARCO POLO Methuen (P); and others.

VAN ALLSBURG, CHRIS
* THE WRECK OF THE ZEPHYR Andersen/Picture Puffin
An old man is sitting by the wreck of a small boat far from the water. How did it get there? Who is the old man? An evocative and suspenseful tale, with unusual but most appropriate illustrations.

VARLEY, SUSAN
* BADGER'S PARTING GIFTS Andersen/Picture Lion
A poignant story of how Badger lives on after his death in the memory of all his friends. Very moving, and sensitively and positively done.

WATTS, BERNADETTE

LITTLE RED RIDING HOOD North–South (H)

A large format retelling of the famous Brothers Grimm story with attractive illustrations and reasonably simple text.

By the same author: THE ELVES AND THE SHOEMAKER North–South (H); VARENKA North–South (H & P); RAPUNZEL North–South (H).

WILDE, OSCAR (Foreman, Michael and Wright, Freire)

* THE SELFISH GIANT Kaye & Ward/Picture Puffin

When the selfish giant refuses to let children play in his garden, the winter persists all year. Not until the giant relents and makes the children welcome again do spring and summer return. A story written more than a hundred years ago, but still fresh and appealing.

WILDSMITH, BRIAN

* PROFESSOR NOAH'S SPACESHIP Oxford University Press (H & P)

The earth becomes so polluted that the animals join Professor Noah in his spaceship, blasting off into space to find another and more congenial world. But when they make a landing they find that they have somehow returned to the earth, hundreds of years ago when everything was fresh and clean. And as the otter says, 'There seems to have been some flooding here'! A delightful modern version of the story of Noah, with wonderful pictures of the animals.

WILKS, MIKE

* THE ULTIMATE ALPHABET BOOK Pavilion (H)

A page for illustrations of objects beginning with each letter of the alphabet. Sounds familiar, but this is an alphabet book with differences! Firstly, there are hundreds (and in one case over a thousand) objects on each page, and secondly, the pictures have been painted with great skill and maturity. In all there are nearly eight thousand objects illustrated. Neither children nor adults will spot them all, but the book is a fascinating test of observational skill.

WILSON, BOB

* STANLEY BAGSHAW AND THE FOURTEEN-FOOT WHEEL Hamish Hamilton/Picture Puffin

Cartoon-style doggerel verse about Stanley's problems with a huge wheel, set in northern parts. Reminiscent of 'The Lion and Albert', but has its own wit and charm. Well done, and excellent for older readers.

In the same series: STANLEY BAGSHAW AND THE TWENTY TWO TON WHALE Hamish Hamilton/Picture Puffin; STANLEY BAGSHAW AND THE MAFEKING SQUARE CHEESE ROBBERY Hamish Hamilton/

Picture Puffin; STANLEY BAGSHAW AND THE SHORT-SIGHTED FOOTBALL TRAINER Hamish Hamilton/Picture Puffin; STANLEY BAGSHAW AND THE RATHER DANGEROUS MIRACLE CURE Hamish Hamilton/Picture Puffin.

YEOMAN, JOHN (Blake, Quentin)
MOUSE TROUBLE Picture Puffin (P)
A farmer, plagued by mice, buys a cat. The cat is so useless that he decides to tie it up in a bag and drown it in the river. But the mice have other ideas! Lively illustrations by the talented Quentin Blake.
By the same author: THE WILD WASHERWOMEN Hamish Hamilton/ Picture Puffin; THE YOUNG PERFORMING HORSE Magnet (P); OUR VILLAGE Walker (H).

APPENDIX 1
THIRTY OUTSTANDING PICTURE BOOKS

Readers who have not used picture books much before may find the following list useful. It consists of some books that I think are outstandingly good; needless to say, there are many more which are of equal or nearly equal quality. All these books are reviewed in earlier chapters. Depending on the age and attainments of the children, a selection of these books could form the core of a classroom collection, to be added to as time, circumstances and finances permit.

For Beginning and Developing Reading

Ahlberg, J. and A., *Each Peach Pear Plum*, Viking Kestrel/Picture Lion.
Ahlberg, J. and A., *The Baby's Catalogue*, Viking Kestrel/Picture Puffin.
Briggs, R., *The Snowman*, Hamish Hamilton/Picture Puffin.
Burningham, J., *Mr Gumpy's Outing*, Cape/Picture Puffin.
Campbell, R., *Dear Zoo*, Campbell Blackie/Picture Puffin.
Carle, E., *The Very Hungry Caterpillar*, Hamish Hamilton/Picture Puffin.
Hill, E., *Where's Spot?*, Heinemann/Picture Puffin.
Hutchins, P., *Rosie's Walk*, Bodley Head/Picture Puffin.
Kuratomi, C., *Mr Bear, Shipwrecked*, Macdonald (H); and series.
Lobel, A., *Frog and Toad Together*, World's Work/Young Puffin; and series.
McKee, D., *Not Now, Bernard*, Andersen/Sparrow.
McKee, D., *King Rollo and the Tree*, Andersen (H); and series.
Nicoll, H. and Pienkowski, J., *Meg and Mog*, Heinemann/Picture Puffin; and series.
Ormerod, J., *Sunshine*, Picture Puffin (P).
Sendak, M., *Where the Wild Things Are*, Bodley Head/Picture Puffin.

For Extending and Independent Reading

Ahlberg, J. and A., *The Jolly Postman*, Heinemann (H).
Ahlberg, J. and A., *Cops and Robbers*, Heinemann/Little Mammoth.
Ahlberg, A., *Mrs Plug the Plumber*, Viking Kestrel/Puffin; and series.
Briggs, R., *Father Christmas*, Hamish Hamilton/Picture Puffin.
Browne, A., *Gorilla*, Julia MacRae/Little Mammoth.

Burningham, J., *Come Away from the Water, Shirley*, Cape/Picture Lion.
Dahl, R., *The Enormous Crocodile*, Cape/Picture Puffin.
Foreman, M., *War and Peas*, Picture Puffin (P).
Hoban, R., *The Rain Door*, Gollancz/Picturemac.
Keeping, C., *The Highwayman*, Oxford University Press (H).
Murphy, J., *On the Way Home*, Macmillan/Picturemac.
Oakley, G., *The Church Mice Adrift*, Macmillan/Picturemac; and series.
Peppe, R., *The Kettleship Pirates*, Viking Kestrel/Picture Puffin; and series.
Pienkowski, J., *Christmas*, Heinemann/Picture Puffin.
Waddell, M., *Going West*, Andersen/Picture Puffin.

APPENDIX 2
PICTURE BOOKS FOR TOPICS

There are huge numbers of picture books about certain topics or featuring certain kinds of character (an almost infinite supply of books about aspects of domestic life, or featuring anthropomorphic bears, pigs or mice, for example). However, with a little exploration, picture books about a wider range of topics can be discovered. The following is by no means an exhaustive list, but it may be helpful in providing starting points for topic work using picture books.

Alphabets

Burningham, J., *Alphabet Book*, Walker (H & P).
Campbell, R., *ABC*, Blackie (H).
Crowther, R., *The Most Amazing Hide-and-Seek Alphabet Book*, Viking Kestrel (H).
Gretz, S., *Teddy Bears ABC*, Black/Picture Lion.
Hughes, S., *Lucy and Tom's ABC*, Gollancz/Picture Puffin.
Pienkowski, J., *ABC*, Heinemann/Picture Puffin.
Wildsmith, B., *ABC*, Oxford University Press (H & P).
Wilks, M., *The Ultimate Alphabet Book*, Pavilion (H).

Babies

Ahlberg, J. and A., *The Baby's Catalogue*, Viking Kestrel/Picture Puffin.
Ahlberg, J. and A., *Burglar Bill*, Heinemann/Little Mammoth.
Brandenburg, F., *Aunt Nina and her Nephews and Nieces* (out of print).
Kerr, J., *Mog and the Baby*, Collins/Picture Lion.
McKee, D., *Who's a Clever Baby Then?*, Andersen/Beaver.
Smith, P., *Jenny's Baby Brother*, Picture Lion (P).
Vipont, E., *The Elephant and the Bad Baby*, Hamish Hamilton/Picture Puffin.
Ziefert, H., *Don't Cry Baby Sam*, Picture Lion (P).

Birds

Andrew, M., *Mac the Macaroni*, Macdonald (H & P).
Bruna, D., *The Little Bird*, Methuen (H).
Crabtree, J., *The Sparrow's Story at the King's Command*, Oxford University Press (H).
Ginsburg, M., *Across the Stream*, Julia MacRae/Picture Puffin.
Hawkins, C. and J., *Jen the Hen*, Piccadily/Picture Puffin.
Hutchins, P., *Rosie's Walk*, Bodley Head/Picture Puffin.
Hutchins, P., *Goodnight, Owl!*, Bodley Head/Picture Puffin.
Kinmonth, P., *Mr Potter's Pigeon*, Pocket Puffin (P).
Pomerantz, C., *One Duck, Another Duck*, Picture Puffin (P).
Tafuri, N., *Have You Seen My Duckling?*, Picture Puffin (P).
Troughton, J., *How the Birds Changed Their Feathers*, Blackie (H).
Zacharias, T. and W., *But Where is the Green Parrot?*, Bodley Head/Picture Piper.

Birthdays

Hill, E., *Spot's Birthday Party*, Heinemann/Picture Puffin.
Hughes, S., *Alfie Gives a Hand*, Bodley Head/Picture Lion.
Hutchins, P., *Happy Birthday, Sam*, Bodley Head/Picture Puffin.
Kuratomi, C., *Mr Bear's Birthday*, Macdonald (H).
Ross, T., *Towser and Sadie's Birthday*, Andersen/Picture Lion.
Zolotow, C., *Mr Rabbit and the Lovely Present*, Bodley Head/Picture Puffin.

Christmas

Briggs, R., *Father Christmas*, Hamish Hamilton/Picture Puffin.
Daly, N., *Leo's Christmas Surprise*, Picture Lion (P).
De Paola, T., *The Christmas Pageant*, Picture Lion (P).
Hill, E., *Spot's First Christmas*, Heinemann/Picture Puffin.
Hughes, S., *Lucy and Tom's Christmas*, Gollancz/Picture Puffin.
Kerr, J., *Mog's Christmas*, Collins/Picture Lion.
Lindgren, A., *Lotta's Christmas Surprise*, Magnet (P).
Moore, C., *The Night Before Christmas*, Orchard (H).
Pienkowski, J., *Christmas*, Heinemann/Picture Puffin.
Stevenson, J., *The Night After Christmas*, Picture Lion (P).
Wildsmith, B., *The Twelve Days of Christmas*, Oxford (P).

Circus

Bruna, D., *Circus*, Methuen (H).
Hill, E., *Spot Goes to the Circus*, Heinemann/Picture Puffin.
Hoff, S., *Julius*, World's Work (H).
Maris, R., *The Punch and Judy Book*, Gollancz/Picture Lion.
Wildsmith, B., *The Circus*, Oxford (H & P).

Colours

Burningham, J., *Colours Book*, Walker (H & P).
Carle, E., *The Mixed-Up Chameleon*, Hamish Hamilton/Picture Puffin.
Duvoisin, R., *See What I Am* (out of print).
Lionni, L., *Little Blue and Little Yellow*, Hodder & Stoughton (H).
Pienkowski, J., *Colours*, Heinemann/Picture Puffin.
Troughton, J. *How the Birds Changed Their Feathers*, Blackie (H).

Dinosaurs

Foreman, M., *Dinosaurs and All That Rubbish*, Picture Puffin (P).
Hoff, S., *Danny and the Dinosaur*, World's Work/Young Puffin.
McCrum, R., *The Brontosaurus Birthday Cake*, Hamish Hamilton/Magnet; and series.
Piers, H., *Long Neck and Thunderfoot*, Viking Kestrel/Picture Puffin.

Fairy Stories

Ahlberg, J. and A., *Each Peach Pear Plum*, Viking Kestrel/Picture Lion.
Ahlberg, J. and A., *The Jolly Postman*, Heinemann (H).
Briggs, R., *The Fairy Tale Treasury*, Picture Puffin (P).
Cole, B., *Princess Smartypants*, Hamish Hamilton/Picture Lion.
Dahl, R., *Revolting Rhymes*, Cape/Picture Puffin.
Lamont, P., *The Troublesome Pig*, Hamish Hamilton/Piccolo.
Ross, T., *The Three Pigs*, Andersen (H); and series.
Watts, B., *Little Red Riding Hood*, North–South (H); and series.

Folk Tales

Aardema, V., *Princess Gorilla and a New Kind of Water*, Bodley Head/Piper; and series.
Cartwright, A., *Norah's Ark*, Hutchinson/Picture Puffin.
De Gerez, T., *Louhi, Witch of the North Farm*, Julia MacRae/Picture Puffin.
French, F., *Rise, Shine!*, Methuen (H).
Keeping C., *Beowulf*, Oxford University Press (P).
Lewis, N., *Cry Wolf and Other Aesop Fables*, Methuen (H).
Longfellow, H., *Hiawatha's Childhood*, Faber/Picture Puffin.
Rose, G., *Wolf! Wolf!* Methuen (H); and series.
Spier, P., *The Book of Jonah*, Hodder & Stoughton (H).
Storr, C., *Androcles and the Lion*, Methuen (P); and series.
Troughton, J., *What Made Tiddalik Laugh*, Blackie (H); and series.

Ghosts, Giants, Monsters, Dragons

Biro, V., *Gumdrop and the Monster*, Picture Puffin (P).
Biro, V., *Drango Dragon*, Ladybird (H).
Briggs, R., *Jim and the Beanstalk*, Picture Puffin (P).

Briggs, R., *Fungus the Bogeyman*, Hamish Hamilton (H & P).
Gage, W., *Mrs Gaddy and the Ghost*, Hippo (P).
Hawkins, C. and J., *Shriek*, Granada (H).
Hutchins, P., *The Very Worst Monster*, Bodley Head/Picture Puffin.
Kent, J., *There's No Such Thing as a Dragon*, Blackie (H & P).
Lingren, A., *The Ghost of Skinny Jack*, Methuen (H).
Mahy, M., *A Lion in the Meadow*, Dent/Picture Puffin.
McKee, D., *Not Now, Bernard*, Andersen/Sparrow.
Murphy, J., *On the Way Home*, Macmillan/Picturemac.
Pienkowski, J., *Haunted House*, Heinemann (H).
Ross, T., *I'm Coming to Get You!*, Andersen/Picture Puffin.
Sendak, M., *Where the Wild Things Are*, Bodley Head/Picture Puffin.
Wilde, O., *The Selfish Giant*, Kaye & Ward/Picture Puffin.

Holidays

Berenstain, S. and J., *The Bear's Holiday*, Collins (H & P).
Briggs, R., *Father Christmas Goes on Holiday*, Hamish Hamilton/Picture Puffin.
Burningham, J., *Come Away from the Water, Shirley*, Cape/Picture Lion.
Goodall, J., *Paddy Pork's Holiday*, Macmillan (H).
Gordon, M., *Frog's Holiday*, Viking Kestrel/Picture Puffin.
Gretz, S., *The Bears Who Went to the Seaside*, Black/Picture Puffin.
Hill, E., *Spot Goes on Holiday*, Heinemann/Picture Puffin.
Hughes, S., *Lucy and Tom at the Seaside*, Gollancz/Corgi.
Pirani, F., *Abigail at the Beach*, Collins/Picture Lion.

Homes

Ahlberg, J, and A., *Peepo!*, Viking Kestrel/Picture Puffin.
Brown, M., *There's No Place Like Home*, Collins (H).
Dupasquier, P., *Our House on the Hill*, Andersen/Picture Puffin.
Pienkowski, J., *Homes*, Heinemann/Picture Puffin.
Roffey, M., *Home Sweet Home*, Bodley Head/Piccolo.
Ziefert, H., *A New House for Mole and Mouse*, Picture Puffin (P).

Illness and Bereavement

Althea, *When Uncle Bob Died*, Dinosaur (P).
Althea, *I Have Eczema*, Dinosaur (P); and series.
Bradman, T. and Browne, E., *Through My Window*, Methuen/Little Mammoth.
Brandenburg, F., *I Don't Feel Well*, Picture Puffin (P).
Burningham, J., *Granpa*, Cape/Picture Puffin.
Janosch, *Little Tiger Get Well Soon!*, Andersen/Hippo.
Keller, H., *Francie's Day in Bed*, Julia MacRae/Hippo.
Varley, S., *Badger's Parting Gifts*, Andersen/Picture Lion.

Journeys

Burningham, J., *Mr Gumpy's Outing*, Cape/Picture Puffin.
Crabtree, J., *The Sparrow's Story at the King's Command*, Oxford University Press (H).
Dupasquier, P., *Dear Daddy . . .*, Andersen/Picture Puffin.
Foreman, M., *Panda's Puzzle and His Voyage of Discovery*, Hamish Hamilton/Pocket Puffin (P).
Ganly, H., *Jyoti's Journey*, Deutsch (H).
Hutchins, P., *Rosie's Walk*, Bodley Head/Picture Puffin.
Prater, J., *The Gift*, Bodley Head/Picture Puffin.
Trotman, F., *The Travels of Marco Polo*, Methuen (P).
Waddell, M., *Going West*, Andersen/Picture Puffin.
Wildsmith, B., *Professor Noah's Spaceship*, Oxford University Press (H & P).

Law and Order

Ahlberg, J. and A., *Cops and Robbers*, Heinemann/Little Mammoth.
Ahlberg, J. and A., *Burglar Bill*, Heinemann/Little Mammoth.
Ahlberg, J., *Mr Creep the Crook*, Viking Kestrel/Puffin.
Keeping, C., *The Highwayman*, Oxford University Press (H).
Lewis, R., *The Great Granny Robbery*, Macdonald (H & P).
Wilson, B., *Stanley Bagshaw and the Mafeking Square Cheese Robbery*, Hamish Hamilton/Picture Puffin.

Multicultural

A number of picture books deal with multicultural issues sensitively and appropriately. The following are examples:

Bradman, T. and Browne, E., *Through My Window*, Methuen/Little Mammoth; and series.
Breinburg, P., *My Brother Sean*, Picture Puffin (P).
Daly, N., *Not So Fast, Songololo*, Gollancz/Picture Puffin.
Ganly, H., *Jyoti's Journey*, Deutsch (H).
Stones, R. and Mann, A., *Mother Goose Comes to Cable Street*, Picture Puffin (P).

Night

Berenstain, S. and J., *Bears in the Night*, Collins (H & P).
Henderson, K., *Fifteen Ways to Go to Bed*, Frances Lincoln (P).
Hutchins, P., *Goodnight, Owl*, Bodley Head/Picture Puffin.
Kerr, J., *Mog in the Dark*, Collins/Picture Lion.
Murphy, J., *Peace at Last*, Macmillan (H & P).
Sendak, M., *In the Night Kitchen*, Bodley Head/Picture Puffin.
Waddell, M., *Can't You Sleep, Little Bear?*, Walker (H).
Ziefert, H., *Nicky's Noisy Night*, Picture Puffin (P).
Ziefert, H., *Say Goodnight*, Picture Puffin (P).

Number

Anno, M., *Anno's Counting Book*, Picturemac (P).
Bang, M., *Ten, Nine, Eight*, Julia MacRae/Picture Puffin.
Bucknall, C., *One Bear All Alone*, Macmillan/Picturemac.
Burningham, J., *Numbers Book*, Walker (H & P).
Crowther, R., *The Most Amazing Hide-and-Seek Counting Book*, Viking Kestrel (H).
Galdone, F., *Over in the Meadow*, Macdonald (H).
Gretz, S., *Teddy Bears 1 to 10*, Picture Lion (P).
Pienkowski, J., *Numbers*, Heinemann/Picture Puffin.
Pomerantz, C., *One Duck, Another Duck*, Picture Puffin (P).
Tafuri, N., *Who's Counting*, Picture Puffin (P).

Nursery Rhymes

Bracken, C., *Little Bo Peep and Other Nursery Rhymes*, Ladybird (H); and series.
Briggs, R., *The Mother Goose Treasury* (out of print).
Galdone, P., *Over in the Meadow*, Macdonald (H); and series.
Lloyd, D., *Over the Moon*, Walker (H & P).
Rosen, M., *We're Going on a Bear Hunt*, Walker (H).
Scarry, R., *Richard Scarry's Best Nursery Rhymes Ever*, Hamlyn (H).
Spier, P., *The Fox Went Out on a Chilly Night*, Doubleday (New York) (H).
Stobbs, W., *This Little Piggy*, Bodley Head; and series.
Stones, R. and Mann, A., *Mother Goose Comes to Cable Street*, Picture Puffin (P).

Pirates

Baum, L., *Juju and the Pirates*, Andersen/Magnet.
Burningham, J., *Come Away from the Water, Shirley*, Cape/Picture Lion.
Hawkins, C. and J., *Pirates*, Collins/Picture Lion.
Hutchings, P., *One Eyed Jake*, Bodley Head/Picture Puffin.
Mahy, M., *The Man Whose Mother was a Pirate*, Dent/Picture Puffin.
Peppe, R., *The Kettleship Pirates*, Viking Kestrel/Picture Puffin.
Ryan, J., *Captain Pugwash and the Midnight Feast*, Young Puffin (P); and series.
Sefton, C., *The Ghost-Ship*, Hamish Hamilton (H).

Relations

Baum, L., *Are We Nearly There?*, Bodley Head/Magnet.
Blume, J., *The Pain and the Great One*, Heinemann/Piper.
Cole, B., *The Trouble with Dad*, Heinemann/Picture Lion; and series.
De Paola, T., *Nana Upstairs and Nana Downstairs*, Methuen (H).
Dupasquier, P., *Dear Daddy ...*, Andersen/Picture Puffin.
Hawkins, C. and J., *The Granny Book*, Picture Lion (P).
Oxenbury, H., *Gran and Grandpa*, Walker (H & P).
Sowter, N., *Maisie Middleton*, Picture Lion (P).

School

Ahlberg, J., *Mr Tick the Teacher*, Viking Kestrel/Puffin.
Breinburg, P., *My Brother Sean*, Picture Puffin (P).
Hill, E., *Spot Goes to School*, Heinemann/Picture Puffin.
Howe, J., *The Day the Teacher Went Bananas*, Viking Kestrel/Picture Puffin.
Hughes, S., *Lucy and Tom Go to School*, Gollancz/Carousel.
Rayner, M., *Crocodarling*, Collins/Picture Lion.
Scarry, R., *Great Big Schoolhouse*, Collins (H).
Wilmer, D., *The Playground*, Collins (H & P).

Sea

Ahlberg, J., *Master Salt the Sailor's Son*, Viking Kestrel/Puffin.
Ardizzone, E., *Tim's Last Voyage*, Picturemac (P).
Armitage, R. and D., *The Lighthouse Keeper's Lunch*, Deutsch/Picture Puffin; and series.
Biro, V., *Gumdrop at Sea*, Hodder & Stoughton (H).
Collington, P., *Little Pickle*, Methuen/Magnet.
Dupasquier, P., *Jack at Sea*, Heinemann/Picture Puffin.
Kuratomi, C., *Mr Bear, Shipwrecked*, Macdonald (H).
Nicoll, H., *Meg at Sea*, Heinemann/Picture Puffin.

Shopping

Armitage, R. and D., *Grandma Goes Shopping*, Deutsch/Picture Puffin.
Burningham, J., *The Shopping Basket*, Cape/Picture Lion.
Daly, N., *Not So Fast, Songololo*, Gollancz/Picture Puffin.
Garland, S., *Going Shopping*, Bodley Head/Picture Puffin.
Gordon, M., *Wilberforce Goes Shopping*, Viking Kestrel/Picture Puffin.
Gretz, S., *Teddybears Go Shopping*, Black/Hippo.
Hutchins, P., *Don't Forget the Bacon*, Bodley Head/Picture Puffin.
Vipont, E., *The Elephant and the Bad Baby*, Hamish Hamilton/Picture Puffin.

Time

Burningham, J., *Seasons*, Cape (H).
Carle, E., *The Bad Tempered Ladybird*, Hamish Hamilton/Picture Puffin.
Hawkins, C., *Mr Wolf's Week*, Heinemann/Picture Lion.
Hawkins, C., *What's the Time Mr Wolf?*, Heinemann/Picture Lion.
Hughes, S., *Lucy and Tom's Day*, Gollancz/Picture Puffin.
Hutchins, P., *Clocks and More Clocks*, Bodley Head/Picture Puffin.
Lobel, A., *Frog and Toad All Year*, World's Work/Young Puffin.
Murphy, J., *Peace at Last*, Macmillan (H & P).
Murphy, J., *Five Minutes Peace*, Walker (H & P).
Ormerod, J., *Sunshine*, Picture Puffin (P).
Pienkowski, J., *Time*, Heinemann/Picture Puffin.

Weather

Briggs, R., *The Snowman*, Hamish Hamilton/Picture Puffin.
Briggs, R., *Father Christmas*, Hamish Hamilton/Picture Puffin.
Cresswell, H., *The Weather Cat*, Collins (H & P).
Hutchins, P., *The Wind Blew*, Bodley Head/Picture Puffin.
Nicoll, H., *Mog in the Fog*, Heinemann/Picture Puffin.
Pienkowski, J., *Weather*, Heinemann/Picture Puffin.
Spier, P., *Rain*, Collins (H).

Witches

Bird, M., *The Witch's Handbook*, Beaver (P).
Brown, M., *Witches Four*, Hamish Hamilton/Picture Corgi.
De Gerez, T., *Louhi, Witch of the North Farm*, Julia MacRae/Picture Puffin.
Falconer, E., *Three Little Witches*, Orchard/Picture Lion.
Hawkins, C. and J., *Witches*, Granada/Picture Lion.
Nicoll, H., *Meg and Mog*, Heinemann/Picture Puffin; and series.

Zoos

Browne, A., *Gorilla*, Julia MacRae/Little Mammoth
Campbell, R.; *Dear Zoo*, Campbell/Blackie.
Hersom, K., *Maybe it's a Tiger*, Picturemac (P).
Nicoll, H., *Mog at the Zoo*, Heinemann/Picture Puffin; and series.
Pienkowski, J., *Zoo*, Heinemann/Picture Puffin.
Willis, J., *The Tale of Fearsome Fritz*, Andersen/Beaver.

BIBLIOGRAPHY

This bibliography includes some interesting books relating to older children, but most focus mainly on young children. An asterisk (*) denotes a particularly recommended book.

Teaching and Learning Reading

Arnold, H., *Listening to Children Reading*, Sevenoaks, Hodder & Stoughton, 1982.
Beard, R. *Developing Reading 3–13*, London, Hodder & Stoughton, 1987.
* Bennett, J., *Learning to Read With Picture Books* (3rd edn), Stroud, Thimble Press, 1985.
* Branston, P. and Provis, M., *Children and Parents Enjoying Reading*, London, Hodder & Stoughton, 1986.
Butler, D. and Clay, M., *Reading Begins at Home*, London, Heinemann, 1979.
McKenzie, M., *Journeys into Literacy*, Huddersfield, Schofield & Sims, 1986.
* Meek, M., *Learning to Read*, London, Bodley Head, 1982.
Meek, M. and Mills, C. (eds.), *Language and Literacy in the Primary School*, Lewes, Falmer Press, 1988.
* Moon, C. (ed.), *Practical Ways to Teach Reading*, London, Ward Lock, 1985.
Smith, F., *Reading* (2nd edn), Cambridge University Press, 1985.
* Waterland, L., *Read With Me* (2nd edn), Stroud, Thimble Press, 1988.

Choosing and Using Children's Books

Benton, M. and Fox, G., *Teaching Literature Nine to Fourteen*, Oxford University Press, 1985.
Butler, D., *Cushla and Her Books*, Hodder & Stoughton, 1979/Harmondsworth, Penguin, 1980.
* Butler, D., *Babies Need Books*, Bodley Head, 1980/Harmondsworth, Penguin, 1981.
Butler, D., *Five to Eight*, London, Bodley Head, 1986.
Cass, J., *Literature and the Young Child* (2nd edn), Harlow, Longman, 1984.
Chambers, A., *Introducing Books to Children*, London, Heinemann, 1983.
* Heeks, P., *Choosing and Using Books in the First School*, London, Macmillan, 1981.
* Hoffman, M. *et al.* (eds.), *Children, Language and Literature*, Milton Keynes, Open University Press, 1983.
Hollindale, P., *Choosing Books for Children*, London, Paul Elek, 1974.
McKenzie, M. and Warlow, A., *Reading Matters*, London, Hodder & Stoughton, 1977.

APPENDIX 3
EASY PICTURE BOOKS FOR OLDER READERS

Although many of the books reviewed in Chapter 11 are suitable for older readers, the following authors have produced picture books that may be particularly useful for maintaining the interest of older children who find reading difficult. Much of the work of these authors has a fairly high interest level, but either a relatively straightforward text or a strip cartoon format (which provides plenty of support).

Anno, M.: e.g. *Anno's Counting Book*, Picturemac (P).
Blake, Q.: e.g. *Mr Magnolia*, Cape/Picture Lion.
Briggs, R.: e.g. *Jim and the Beanstalk*, Picture Puffin (P).
Browne, A.: e.g. *A Walk in the Park*, Hamish Hamilton/Picturemac.
Dupasquier, P.: e.g. *Jack at Sea*, Andersen/Picture Puffin.
Foreman, M.: e.g. *Dinosaurs and All That Rubbish*, Picture Puffin (P).
Goscinny, R.: e.g. *Asterix in Britain*, Hodder & Stoughton (H & P).
Hawkins, C. and J.: e.g. *Shriek*, Granada (H).
Herge: e.g. *The Adventures of Tintin: Prisoners of the Sun*, Methuen (H & P).
Hoban, R.: e.g. *The Rain Door*, Gollancz/Picturemac.
Hoff, S.: e.g. *Stanley*, Heinemann (P).
McNaughton, C.: e.g. *Football Crazy*, Heinemann/Little Mammoth.
Waddell, M.: e.g. *Going West*, Andersen/Picture Puffin.
Wilson, B.: e.g. *Stanley Bagshaw and the Fourteen-Foot Wheel*, Hamish Hamilton/Picture Puffin.

Moss, E., *Picture Books for Young People 9–13* (2nd edn), Stroud, Thimble Press, 1988.
Protherough, R., *Developing Response to Fiction*, Milton Keynes, Open University Press, 1983.
Short, H., *Bright Ideas: Using Books in the Classroom*, Leamington Spa, Scholastic Publications, 1989.
Taylor, B. and Braithwaite, P., *The Good Book Guide to Children's Books*, Harmondsworth, Penguin, 1987.
* Thomas, R. and Perry, A., *Into Books: 101 Literature Activities for the Classroom*, Melbourne, Oxford University Press, 1984.
Trelease, J., *The Read-Aloud Handbook*, Harmondsworth, Penguin, 1984.
Weir, L., *Telling the Tale: A Storytelling Guide*, Youth Libraries Group, 1988.

Critical Studies

Dixon, B., *Catching Them Young: Vol. 1 Sex Race and Class in Children's Fiction; Vol. 2 Political Ideas in Children's Fiction*, London, Pluto, 1977.
Egoff, S. *et al.* (eds.) *Only Connect: Readings on Children's Literature*, Oxford University Press, 1980.
Inglis, F., *The Promise of Happiness: Value and Meaning in Children's Fiction*, Cambridge University Press, 1981.
Kirkpatrick, D. (ed.) *Twentieth Century Children's Writers*, London, Macmillan, 1983.
Landsberg, M., *The World of Children's Books*, London, Simon & Schuster, 1988.
Leeson, R., *Reading and Righting*, London, Collins, 1985.
Meek, M., *How Texts Teach What Readers Learn*, Stroud, Thimble Press, 1988.
Meek, M. *et al.* (eds.) *The Cool Web: The Pattern of Children's Reading*, London, Bodley Head, 1977.
Rose, J., *The Case of Peter Pan or The Impossibility of Children's Fiction*, London, Macmillan, 1984.
Spink, J., *Children as Readers*, London, Clive Bingley, 1989.
* Townsend, J., *Written for Children* (3rd edn), Harmondsworth, Penguin, 1987.
Tucker, N., *The Child and the Book: A Psychological and Literary Exploration*, Cambridge University Press, 1981.

Research Studies

Chester, T. R., *Children's Books Research: A Practical Guide to Techniques and Sources*, Stroud, Thimble Press, 1989.
Clark, M., *Young Fluent Readers*, London, Heinemann, 1976.
Fry, D., *Children Talk About Books: Seeing Themselves as Readers*, Milton Keynes, Open University Press, 1985.
Ingham, J., *Books and Reading Development: The Bradford Book Flood Experiment*, London, Heinemann, 1981.
Southgate, V. *et al.*, *Extending Beginning Reading*, London, Heinemann, 1981.
Wells, G., *The Meaning Makers: Children Learning Language and Using Language to Learn*, London, Hodder & Stoughton, 1987.
Whitehead, F. *et al.*, *Children and their Books*, London, Macmillan, 1977.

INDEX OF TITLES REVIEWED

INDEX OF AUTHORS AND ILLUSTRATORS

SUBJECT INDEX